Lucretius and the Transpadanes

Lucretius and the Transpadanes

BY LOUISE ADAMS HOLLAND

PRINCETON UNIVERSITY PRESS

PRINCETON, NEW JERSEY

1979

591306

Contents

Preface

After long delay, this small work has been completed only through the devoted assistance of sons and daughters. So I begin by acknowledging my debt to Marian Holland McAllister, to Anésia de Araujo Holland, and to Lawrence Rozier Holland for all they have done to compensate for lost eyesight. Thanks are also owing to the Bryn Mawr College Library and its staff; to my friends Mrs. Virginia Jameson and Mrs. Shirley Mason for providing transportation when I could no longer drive a car; to George Dimock and his family at Smith College who know the secret of banishing despair; to the T.R.S. Broughtons at Chapel Hill; and to Lily Ross Taylor held always in loving memory.

Louise Adams Holland
October 18, 1977

vii

Abbreviations

A.J.P.	*American Journal of Philology*
C.A.H.	*Cambridge Ancient History*
C.J.	*Classical Journal*
C.P.	*Classical Philology*
C.Q.	*Classical Quarterly*
C.R.	*Classical Review*
C.W.	*Classical Weekly (Classical World)*
H.S.C.P.	*Harvard Studies in Classical Philology*
J.R.S.	*Journal of Roman Studies*
P.B.S.R.	*Papers of the British School at Rome*
P.C.A.	*Proceedings of the Classical Association* (London)
P.Q.	*Philological Quarterly*
Rev. Belge	*Revue Belgique*
Riv. Fil.	*Rivista de filosofia*
T.A.P.A.	*Transactions of the American Philological Association*
U. of Cal. St. Cl. Phil.	*University of California Studies in Classical Philology*
Yale Cl. St.	*Yale Classical Studies*

Lucretius and the Transpadanes

I

Regional Differences in Speech

In the absence of tape recordings from antiquity we are woefully ignorant of how classical Latin prose or verse sounded as it was rendered orally. To read verbal descriptions of sounds is a far cry from hearing them, and Quintilian's best efforts sometimes leave us more confused than enlightened. However, we have enough evidence to be sure that the spoken word varied greatly from place to place, no matter how much uniformity the written language maintained.

The *Urbs Roma*, head and heart of the Roman world in law, politics, religion, and warfare, also claimed the cultural leadership, though it produced no city-born writer of distinction except possibly Julius Caesar. We know that for Cicero's generation and its Augustan successors Rome unquestionably set the standard of cultivated speech.[1]

In modern countries, for all the ease and completeness of communication, popular language retains to a surprising degree its local peculiarities. The French of Paris is distinct from that of Bordeaux or Toulouse. The south Italian tendency to drop final vowels balances the inability of some northern Italians to end a word with a consonant.[2] The common expression *piano piano* shortens to *pian piano* or *piano pian* according to latitude.

As for the United States of America, the cultural geographers tell us that radio and television, "though eroding the basic American dialects to some extent,"

3

have so far left them essentially unchanged: "The regional dialects will become less sharply distinguished— but we'll never have uniform speech."[3] Such is the normal variation in countries that claim one national tongue.

Ancient Italy had some special characteristics that tended to emphasize and perpetuate regional traits. Ethnic differences worked with the geographical pockets into which the peninsula naturally divided to set clear lines of separation. One of the many virtues of Salmon's book on the Samnites is the sense it gives of the diversity of the Italian peoples, "with the haphazard timing of their separate migrations, their unequal degree of exposure to foreign influences, the divisive effect of their mountain abodes, and the heterogeneity of the aboriginal populations among whom they settled and whose habits they absorbed."[4]

Though the boundaries between the districts are by no means insurmountable, towns that on a small-scale map look like the closest of neighbors might, for no stronger reason than a stream gulley or a steep little hill, turn their backs on each other and reach out in opposite directions for markets and cult centers. There is a solid geographical reason for the linguistic difference between Ovid's Paelignian forebears and the near-by Frentani,[5] but much less obvious barriers seem equally effective elsewhere.

In every area the artifacts of course change with time, but the regionalism persists and the boundaries remain surprisingly stable. In central Italy, for instance (at least until the imported petrol tin supplanted the native water jar at the town fountain), the one-time domain of the Villanovan urn used a copper pot with high shoulders and neat, brass-collared neck, while the ovoid urn of Latium gave place to a bronze jar with flattened biconical body and flaring rim. The modern forms are in no way

4

derivatives of their ancient predecessors, but those used in one area still differ from those in the next, and the old lines of division endure.

Some of the most important habits that the Latin speakers absorbed from the older inhabitants in various parts of Italy were in their speech, and those not only in words but in accent, intonation, and tempo, which eventually modify words. The racial mixtures we find everywhere in the peninsula are not in themselves important for the history of literature, but the speech differences are reflected at times in the written word, especially in verse structure. We get the impression from Cicero that in his day there were almost as many ways of speaking Latin as there were towns. In the *Brutus* (170f.) he discusses the speech not only of orators but of ordinary citizens from various Italian localities, with their divergence from the true *urbani* of Rome. We learn elsewhere that the Praenestini long maintained their individuality.[6] In Horace's Venusia, one of the largest Latin colonies on record was planted in the midst of Messapians, Oscan-speaking Samnites, and descendants of old Greek settlers to say nothing of a nameless primitive substratum.[7] Those "sons of great centurions" (*Sat.* 1.6, 72f.) who would have continued to be Horace's schoolmates had he remained there, certainly spoke Latin but a Latin that would sound alien to Roman ears.[8]

To take Cicero's native Arpinum as another example, the town was originally Volscian, overlaid with a fresh touch of Oscan when the Samnites absorbed it for a while in the fourth century. Then it was annexed by Rome, at first "sine suffragio," but finally with full citizenship in 188 B.C.[9] The official language had been Latin for a long time before Cicero was born, but the manner of speaking it could hardly fail to reflect other strains.

5

The Latin of such a place, however correct, might declare
its origin to Roman purists wherever they heard it. One
might wonder if a hint of Arpinum came out occasionally in Cicero's own inflection, though he would be
the last to realize it. In the *Pro Sulla* 6.24, when he re-
proaches Manlius Torquatus for branding his consulship
the rule of an alien, there is no mention of language, but
the true Roman ear of a Torquatus might have caught
something to play upon at the trial, something such as
showed the old market woman that Theophrastus was no
Athenian born.[10] On the possible exploitation in the
courtroom of personal peculiarities, Cicero himself says
(*De Orat.* II.243) "—imitatione brevi iniecta, in aliquo
insigni ad irridendum vitio reperiantur."[a]

It was possibly to insure his sons against provincialism
that Cicero's father began while Marcus and Quintus
were still children to transfer his household to Rome for
at least part of the year. Even there, however, the boys
were under the unbroken influence of the family and the
family servants in their house on the Carinae, though they
had ampler advantages than Arpinum could offer in
schools and in the tutelage of such cosmopolitan teachers
as Archias (*Pro Archia* I).

The common custom of going to Rome to study missed
some of its potential leveling effect because of a natural
inclination to consort with one's own kind. When
Horace's father removed him from Venusia to Rome, he
chose for his teacher Orbilius of Beneventum, who was
hardly one to spoil his southern accent but who may
have helped to establish in Horace's mind a rooted dislike
for the Cisalpines (Horace, *Ep.* II.1.70; *Sat.* I.10.36ff., 47;

[a] ". . . that by the introduction of a slight touch of mimicry
they are found out in some fault noticeable enough to raise a
laugh."

II.5.41). Similarly, while Virgil was studying with Siro near Naples, he lived with a group of northerners like himself.[11]

Naturally the speech of provincials outside of Italy showed even more conspicuous peculiarities. Cicero characterizes the language of Corduba in Spain as *pingue* and *peregrinum* (*Pro Archia* 261), a comment in line with Messala's acid remark (Seneca, *Cont.* II.12) about Porcius Latro, a distinguished son of that province: "Sua lingua disertus est."[b] Cicero was of course aware of the large numbers of Italians who had settled in Spain during the two centuries before his time, but he was spared the knowledge of that great backwash of Spaniards over the Roman world of letters in the first century of the Empire. One of their number was the famous Quintilian, whose dicta about sound and accent, except for what he drew directly from Cicero, we might well beware of accepting too uncritically. It may be, as is generally assumed, that he spent an interval of his boyhood in Rome under Roman instruction, but, if so, nobody knows when or for how long.[12] His contacts with well-known teachers and orators in Rome belong to a later stage of his education. He had certainly lived in Spain and was well known there for some time before A.D. 68, when Galba assigned him to a post as a professor of rhetoric in Rome.[13] He thus followed in the steps of his fellow Spaniard, Porcius Latro, as a teacher in the capital. It would be a miracle if Quintilian's own Latin had no foreign color that such critics as Pollio and Messala would have observed instantly,[14] and if his ear was perfectly attuned to judge of what he heard in Italy. He himself says (I.1.5): "Et natura tenacissimi sumus eorum quae rudibus annis per-

---

[b] "He is eloquent in his own language."

cepimus; ut sapor, quo nova imbuas, durat, nec lanarum colores quibus simplex ille candor mutatus est, elui possunt. Et haec ipsa magis pertinaciter haerent, quo deteriora sunt.—Non assuescat ergo, ne dum infans quidem est, sermoni qui dediscendus sit."[c] Quintilian has expanded this passage from a single sentence in Cicero (*Brutus* 210): "Sed magni interest quos quisque audiat cotidie domi, quibuscum loquatur a puero, quem ad modum patres, paedagogi, matres etiam loquantur."[d]

It is possible that Quintilian was not sensitive to the degree in which the Latin of other towns might differ in sound from that of Rome. He brushes aside rather impatiently the regional peculiarities that had been commonly observed (1.5.56): "Taceo de Tuscis et Sabinis et Praenestinis quoque: nam ut eorum sermone utentem Vettium Lucilius insectatur, quemadmodum Pollio deprehendit in Livio Patavinitatem, licet omnia Italica pro Romanis habeam."[e] His interest is in the ideas conveyed by words rather than in their sound, or even in the supplementary meanings their sounds may suggest. When he re-used Cicero's anecdote about Theophrastus (*Brutus*

[c] "And we are by nature most tenacious of childish impressions, just as the flavor first absorbed by vessels when new persists, and the colour imparted by dyes to the primitive whiteness of wool is indelible. Further, it is the worst impressions that are most durable. . . . Do not, therefore, allow the boy to become accustomed even in infancy to a style of speech which he will subsequently have to unlearn." Butler.

[d] "It does certainly make a great difference with what sort of speakers one is daily associated at home, with whom one has been in the habit of talking from childhood, how one's father, one's attendant, one's mother too, speak." Hendrickson.

[e] "I pass over Tuscan, Sabine, or Praenestine, for though Lucilius attacks Vettius for using their speech, and Pollio censured a Patavian quality in Livy, I may be allowed to regard all Italic speech as Roman."

8

172) he spoiled the point by making the old market woman notice the strangeness of a single word ("annotata unius affectatione verbi"),[15] rather than the total color and tone of the man's speech, as in Cicero's version. "Sic, ut opinor, in nostris est quidam urbanorum sicut illic Atticorum sonus."[f]

A passage in the *Institutes* (XI.3. 30) is often cited to show Quintilian's interest in sound: "—urbanum, id est in quo nulla neque rusticitas neque peregrinitas resonet."[g] This is an echo of Cicero and uses his language, though *urbanus* had surely lost much of its Republican meaning before Quintilian's time, and Cicero would use *rusticus* and *peregrinus* rather than those awkward abstracts. *Resono* is Cicero's term in discussing the "ring" or "intonation" of the speaker's voice (e.g. *Brutus* 171; *Orator* 150, 161).

Quintilian condemns onomatopeia (1.5.72) in a way that indicates a general dislike of imitative sounds in language. This is natural in one who is not vividly aware, as the north Italian poets were, of the sounds of words with all their rich possibilities of suggestion.[16] To a Quintilian, onomatopeia and other sound effects might well seem an irrelevance that interfered with his direct reception of the idea to be communicated. His insensitivity to sound effects[17] adequately explains his casual treatment of Catullus, whom, though he refers to him several times, he does not consider important in the lyric; and even of Lucretius (X.1.87) for all his effective borrowing of the honey on the rim (III.1.4).[18] It also ac-

---

[f] "In like manner I take it there is in our urban speakers a characteristic accent analogous to that peculiar to Athens." Hendrickson.

[g] "urbane, that is, of a style with no ring of the countrified provincial."

counts for his unqualified enthusiasm for Horace, whose
appeal is directly to the mind through the meaning and
arrangement of words with little dependence on sound
and rhythm.[19] Quintilian's fine comment on Horace's
gifts (x.1.96) is familiar: "At Lyricorum idem Horatius
fere solus legi dignus. Nam et insurgit aliquando et plenus
est iucunditatis et gratiae et variis figuris et verbis feli-
cissime audax."[h]

Almost as completely detached as Spain from Cicero's
usual associations was the wide valley of the Po and its
sub-Alpine reaches, the tenth Roman province, Gallia
Cisalpina.[20] Those lands, acquired from a mixed popula-
tion of Gauls, Ligurians, and other tribes, including even
a few Etruscans, had been available for Latin colonies
and for distribution *viritim* to Italians disturbed by Hannibal's destructive passing and by all the changes and
troubles of the following century.[21] The soil was fertile,
the water supply abundant. The settlers prospered. Sub-
stantial towns developed, connected by navigable rivers
and by a network of roads.[22] They were too far from
Roman markets to send them much in the early days
except the acorn-fed swine Polybius mentions (ii.15).
These, like herds of stringy turkeys one meets nowadays
on the Greek roads, could travel on their own power,
and they helped to feed the capital and the Roman armies.
By Strabo's time, however, trade with Rome in manu-
factured articles was flourishing.[23] Well-to-do, if not
wealthy, families developed a class with time to devote
to the life of the mind. They were far enough removed
to escape most of those disorders that afflicted the penin-

[h] "But of the lyric poets Horace is likewise almost the only
one worth reading. For he rises to heights at times and is full of
charm and grace and is most happily daring in various words
and figures."

sula during the Social and Civil Wars.[24] What we have
left of Suetonius gives us a tantalizing glimpse of schools
and scholars in Gallia. Apparently, ambitious parents
need not hurry their sons off to Rome for education when
so much was available nearer home. Virgil found his
schooling first at Cremona and later at Mediolanum.[25]

Nobody can fail to be impressed by the number of
writers that Gallia produced. Some of the poets and
critics[26] known to us from repeated citations are Valerius
Cato, Quintilius Varus, Helvius Cinna, Alfenus Varus,
Furius Bibaculus, and Varro of Atax, while in the field
of prose Livy is a host in himself. Catullus refers to the
older members of the group, and the unwilling testimony
of Horace (cf. *Sat.* 1.10) gives evidence of their continued
importance in the following generation. Most of the
Transpadani would be little more than names to us if
Catullus had not survived in a single manuscript[27] to tell
us both by his own poems and by what he says of his
contemporaries something of the themes they treated
and even of their style.

The pioneers had brought with them to the north,
along with their archaic Latin, a strong element of
Oscan. In the Po Valley they lived among barbarian
languages and dialects. Frank notes that half a dozen
languages were spoken in the Verona of Catullus's
youth.[28] The displacement of the earlier populations
throughout the province may not have been as sweeping
as has usually been assumed. Strabo (v.1.6) calls Mediolanum the metropolis of the Insubrians. Though the de-
feat and expulsion of the Boii has been thought complete,
remnants probably survived along the Via Aemilia.[29]
Latin speakers borrowed some words outright from the
Gauls, notably terms for horses and horse-drawn ve-
hicles.[30] From their motley background the dwellers in

the valley apparently became a people of nimble tongues with a special facility in handling open vowel junctions, and making literary capital of the little rippling breaks they made in verse without destroying the metrical form, as a vagrant breeze may stir thousands of tiny ripples on the surface of ocean swells without in the least affecting the motion of the great rollers beneath. This is one feature that made it possible for Catullus to use the simplest of schemes to express a surprising variety of mood and feeling.[31]

Cicero knew the characteristic *sonus* of northern speech, and thoroughly disliked it. When Brutus, the governor designate of Gallia Cisalpina, was planning to set out for his province, Cicero warned him to watch out for his Latin. It would risk corruption there, not so much from particular words and phrases, which could be "unlearned," as from an alien tone and inflection (*Brutus* 171): "Illud est maius, quod in vocibus nostrorum oratorum retinnit quiddam et resonat urbanius. Nec hoc in oratoribus modo apparet sed etiam in ceteris."[i] According to Cicero, any untrained Roman speaks more pleasingly than cultivated gentlemen from other towns (*De Orat.* iii.43): "Nostri minus student litteris quam Latini, tamen ex istis quos nostis urbanis in quibus minimum est litterarum nemo est quin litteratissimum togatorum omnium Q. Valerium Soranum lenitate vocis atque ipso oris pressu et sono facile vincat."[j]

---

[i] "It is much more significant that in the words and pronunciation of our orators there is a certain intonation and quality that is characteristic of the city, and this is recognizable not in orators only but in others."

[j] "Our citizens study literature less than the Latins (this includes the northern colonies), and yet there is not one of your acquaintance in the city, virtually devoid as they are of literature, who does not easily best Q. Valerius Soranus, the most

Roman usage is the correct usage.[32] Though Cicero considers all places outside the capital inferior, he singles out Gallia for special censure more than once. In his vitriolic attack on Calpurnius Piso, he makes a point of the allegation that Piso was born at Placentia on the Po and that his maternal grandfather was an Insubrian.[33] Cicero enjoys recounting an anecdote in which a man of Placentia is worsted in a contest of wits by a Roman crier (*Brutus* 172). He accuses the playwright Caecilius, in origin an Insubrian, of using bad Latin: "Malus enim auctor Latinitatis est."[34] All that made the Gallic speech objectionable to Cicero we can not expect to know exactly, though he gives us some indications in his rhetorical works. Even he is frustrated by what seems to be the positive side of the question, and finds it easier to say what he dislikes in diction than to explain the qualities of the *urbanitas* he admires (*Brutus* 171): "Et Brutus 'Qui est', inquit, 'iste tandem urbanitatis color?' 'Nescio', inquam, 'tantum esse quendam scio. Id tu, Brute, iam intelleges, cum in Galliam veneris.' "[k]

As to what Cicero disliked in diction, we hear harshness and roughness mentioned, and a disagreeable clashing of consonants,[35] but apparently worst of all to him is the effect he calls *hiulcans*, "gaping," i.e. open vowel junctions such as occur in hiatus or elision. The frequency of such *concursus* in Gallic usage he judges a serious fault. He vividly characterizes such sounds as *vastae*, or *hiantes*, "open-mouthed," and says no Roman

erudite *littérateur* of all (outsiders) who hold the citizenship, in smoothness of voice and in neatness and clearness of diction."

[k] " 'What do you mean by an urban colouring?' asked Brutus. 'I can't exactly say,' I replied, 'I only know that it exists. You will understand what I mean, Brutus, when you come into Gaul.' " Hendrickson.

would be "tam rusticus" as to fail to avoid them by running the words together.[36] We can hardly say with con-
fidence how such combinations were treated in ordinary
conversation or in reading prose, but in verse, except for
the clear separation of hiatus, which is comparatively
rare,[37] there results an extra-rhythmic beat, a syllable not
counted in the metrical pattern and which must be
dropped entirely in reading, or slurred, or read in clipped
time like the dactyls in hendecasyllabics. In their ways of
using or avoiding elision, the poets of the Ciceronian and
Augustan times differ from one another more in accordance with their geographical origins than with their
chronological places in the list. Cicero rightly insists that
the ear must be the judge,[38] but the judgment of the ear
depends upon experience of sound, which is not the same
in all parts of the country. His own ear prefers a strong,
regular beat in verse, and he would permit as few breaks
as are possible in a language like Latin without producing
a stiff and unnatural effect. His attitude obviously differs
from that of Catullus and his *conterranei*, but Horace, the
Roman-trained southerner, is in Cicero's camp. In fact
it seems possible to determine a poet's native region, when
it is otherwise unknown, by his avoidance of elision, or
by his exploitation of it as a useful literary device. In his
use of elision, Lucretius, for example, belongs, as I shall
try to show, in the north with Catullus and Virgil rather
than in Cicero's Rome.

We know from Cicero's works that in the rhythms of
prose (*Orator* 195ff., esp. 198), which are so much more
subtle and difficult than those of verse because in prose
there is no possibility of following an established pattern,
his ear was sensitive and his artistry superb. Some of his
noble cadences seem to have touched the responsive
imagination of Virgil[39] and perhaps helped to form the

concept of the *Aeneid*. In contrast to his mastery over prose, Cicero's feeling for verse rhythms is surprisingly limited.[40] He did, to be sure, contribute to the development of the Latin hexameter by his careful workmanship, but except for a few short pieces of translation used in his essays, his efforts were spent on subjects that might well have been treated in prose. A statement of his is recorded in Seneca (*Ep.* 49.51): "Negat Cicero si duplicetur sibi aetas, habiturum se tempus quo legat lyricos."[1] Another revealing remark in his own *Orator* (183f.) tells us all we need to know about his response to such works: "sed in versibus res est apertior, quamquam etiam a modis quibusdam cantu remoto soluta esse videatur oratio maximeque id in optimo quoque eorum poetarum qui λυρικοί a Graecis nominantur, quos cum cantu spoliaveris, nuda paene remanet oratio. Quorum similia sunt quaedam etiam apud nostros,—."[m]

A free use of open vowel junctions was banned in the style of Roman speech Cicero praises as possessing the quality of *urbanitas*. Their effect was to keep the mouth open between words or syllables in a manner he found unpleasant, though he observes with wonder that the Greeks seem to like it (*Orator* 152): "Sed Graeci viderint: nobis ne si cupiamus quidem distrahere voces conceditur."[n] Cicero himself used hiatus only once in his trans-

---

[1] "Cicero says that if he were given a second life to live, he would have no time for reading lyric poets."

[m] "But in poetry the presence of rhythm is more obvious, although in certain metres, if the musical accompaniment be taken away, the words seem to lack rhythm; this is particularly true of the best of the poets whom the Greeks call 'lyric'; deprive them of the musical accompaniment and almost nothing but bare prose remains. We have something like this at times in Latin poetry. . . ." Hubbell.

[n] "But let the Greeks look to their own practice: we are not

lation of *Aratus*,[41] and that reproduced one in the original Greek. "Hoc idem nostri saepius non tulissent, quod Graeci laudare etiam solent." (*Orator* 153)[o]

In Cicero's view the people who speak best are those residents of the city who have the polish and *suavitas* of the capital (*Brutus* 258): "Sed omnes tum fere, qui neque extra urbem hanc vixerant neque eos aliqua barbaries domestica infuscaverat, recte loquebantur."[p] Roman ladies, he says, should follow the example of such worthies as Laelia and Cornelia, and form their children's speech by close personal care of them.[42]

Cicero's comments show that the speech he approves as truly Roman flows in sequences smooth and neatly joined[43] and with a pronunciation to which he applies the expressive adverb *presse*, in contrast to such epithets as *hians, hiulcus, vastus*, which he attaches to a way of speaking he considers more vulgar than *urbanus*.[44] However, those open vowel junctions he prefers to avoid are natural to the Latin language with its inflected endings and were common in everyday talk. Even in literary compositions they had their uses, as Cicero realizes,[45] in imparting an air of easy informality. Lucilius gave a colloquial tone to his satires by using them freely. For the same reason Horace's satires, which he himself calls "sermones" ("chats"), show many elisions,[46] while the Odes with their careful literary finish have few, or in some cases none at all. Complete elimination of elision in

---

allowed to make a pause between vowels, even if we should wish to do so."

[o] "Our poets would not have permitted this very often, but the Greeks are accustomed even to praise it."

[p] "In the old days almost everybody, who had not lived much outside the city and whom no barbarous taint in the household affected, spoke correctly."

a Latin poem of more than a few lines is a *tour de force* that could only be achieved by painstaking attention to the choice and arrangement of words.[47]

In his avoidance of elision Ovid even goes beyond the Ciceronian-Horatian standard. The few he uses are too light to interrupt the smooth swiftness of his lines. Occasionally he finds them convenient, but nowhere does he show an interest in their expressive power, which is so noteworthy in Catullus, Lucretius, and Virgil.[48] His attitude toward elision is especially evident in the changes he makes in lines borrowed from those northerners, changes not intended to make the passages his own, for he has not the slightest objection to transferring bodily the most famous phrases when they fit his rules. Doubtless he enjoyed preparing a shock for the reader who came upon Horace's "splendidior vitro" in Polyphemus's praise of Galatea (*Met.* xiii.791); or even more unexpectedly, the Sybil's warning to Aeneas (*Aen.* vi.129), "Hoc opus, hic labor est," applied to the difficulty of arranging an assignation without paying for it (*A.A.* 1.453).[49] But several elisions in one line are too many for his taste, and he sometimes disposes of breaks in the original by clever little shifts in vocabulary. So Catullus 62.42 and 44:

Multi illum pueri, multae optavere puellae.

. . . . . .

Nulli illum pueri, nullae optavere puellae.

became in Ovid, *Met.* iii.353 and 355:

Multi illum iuvenes, multae cupiere puellae.

. . . . . .

Nulli illum iuvenes, nullae tetigere puellae.

Virgil's hesitant shepherd (*Ec.* ii.25f.):

17

Nec sum adea informis: nuper me in litore vidi
Cum placidum ventis staret mare,[q]

while in Ovid (*Met.* XIII.840f.) the shaggy, one-eyed
Polyphemus confidently announces:

Certe ego me novi liquidaeque in imagine vidi
Nuper aquae,—placuitque mihi mea forma videnti.[r]

It seems as clear that we should drop Ovid's elisions of
short final *E* as that we should retain every syllable of
Virgil. As in Horace's "Dulce et decorum est pro patria
mori," Ovid's elisions may be dropped with impunity.[50]

Such places remind us that the statistical method of
studying elision is of limited usefulness, since the question
is not so much, "How many?" as "What kind?" and
every case should be considered in its context with due
attention to theme and mood. As the south Italians ignore
the loss of their word endings today, the ancients accustomed to such omissions would be indifferent to the
complete suppression of occasional syllables. In some
districts it seems to have been the practice to drop the
extra-rhythmic element and follow Cicero's injunction to
coniungere voces, but in others, where a nimble tongue
and a practiced ear made it possible, every hemi-demi-
semi-quaver was pronounced.[51] It must have been
almost impossibly difficult for anyone not himself a
northerner to meet such a requirement. Little wonder
that Virgil preferred to read his own works. To share
the sustained effort of reading the four books of the
Georgics to Augustus, he enlisted no less a personage than

---

[q] "I am not so ill-favored: lately I saw my reflection near the
shore when the sea was undisturbed by the wind."

[r] "Surely I know what I look like and I saw myself lately in a
reflection in the clear water and my appearance was pleasing to
me when I saw it."

Maecenas (Suetonius, *Vergil* 27), who was enough of a northerner to cope with Virgil's meter. No wonder that it was the Umbrian Propertius who first acclaimed the forthcoming *Aeneid* as something *"maius Iliade"*[52] or that Horace the southerner, while expressing warm affection and admiration for Virgil as a person, nowhere registers enthusiasm for his poems.[53]

So the old debate on how elisions should be read[54] turns out to be like the Caucus Race in "Alice" where all have won and all must have prizes. The question was a regional one. Naturally writers who thought in terms of dropping elisions would tend to limit their use both in number and in kind. There seems to have been a fairly definite line of division, a sort of linguistic Mason and Dixon Line, at about the latitude of Rome, or perhaps along the hills and ridges on the Tuscan-Umbrian side of the Tiber, to separate the eliders from the non-eliders. Cicero states the case for the writers of his persuasion who preferred to admit only the easiest elisions and to avoid them as far as possible (*Orator* 150-52): "Nam ut in legendo oculus, sic animus in dicendo prospiciet quid sequatur, ne extremorum verborum cum sequentibus primis concursus aut hiulcas voces efficiat aut asperas. Quamvis enim suaves gravesque sententiae, tamen, si inconditis verbis efferantur, offendent auris quarum est iudicium superbissimum."[8] Cicero evidently considers a sequence with noticeable open junctions "ill-arranged"

---

[8] "For as the eye looks ahead in reading, so in speaking the mind will foresee what is to follow, so that the juxtaposition of the final syllable with the initial may not cause harsh or gaping sounds. For however agreeable or important thoughts may be, still if they are expressed in words which are ill-arranged, they will offend the ear which is very fastidious in its judgement." Hubbell.

and lays it down as a law that one should run such words together, "vocalis coniungere" (*Orator* 150). The deliberate use of elision by the northern writers as an effective means of expression was dismissed by the Roman school as rustic carelessness. It was certainly no "conspiracy of silence" that explains the Roman neglect of Catullus and Lucretius in their lifetime.[55] It was rather an understandable failure on the part of the hard-pressed Romans in the capital to find time in their chronic insecurity to acquire an appreciation of provincial writers with what seemed to them uncouth tricks of style. If we remember that the reading of a classical poem was not a silent perusal, but a "live" performance, we can imagine the destructive effect of taking verses written by a Cisalpine and reading them with a correct Roman accent, firm, crisp and clear-cut, with all elisions dropped for the sake of "joining the vowels." Hendrickson has well said, "There must have been much in the language of the brilliant group of poets from north Italy to offend the Roman ear and lay them open to the charge of provincialism and defective Latinity."[56]

In the next generation, Virgil, the Mantuan, with patrons so highly placed as to make his position unassailable, maintained his northern speech habits, somewhat softened but basically the same. In the matter of open vowel junctions he is as different from Horace as Catullus and Lucretius are different from Cicero. He was not only able to hold his own (the *Aeneid* has more elisions than the *Eclogues*), but he provided the bridge by which his *conterranei*, Catullus and Lucretius, entered into what post-mortem recognition they won in the Augustan era.

II

Catullus: Northern Characteristics

Not even his long-time friend and compatriot, Cornelius Nepos, set down the life story of Catullus while the facts were readily available. Except for Ovid's reference (*Am.* III.9.62) to his having died young, and the priceless note in Suetonius[1] on his contacts with Julius Caesar, all modern knowledge of Catullus as an individual depends on what he reveals of himself in his poems. We have no exact dates for the beginning and end of his short life. We know that he came from Verona, deep in the heart of the Gallia Cisalpina that Cicero so much disliked.[2] His father was well enough placed both socially and financially to play host to Caesar when the governor's duties took him to Verona.[3] It seems a reasonable conjecture that the son of such a family was first tutored at home, and later sent to one of the Gallic centers of scholarship. Probably in his case it was to a school at Cremona where the young Virgil followed him in the next generation and acquired the intimate familiarity with the poems of Catullus so evident in his own writings. In that same school Quintilius Varus linked the two generations by his friendships in both.[4]

There is no evidence that Catullus went to Rome before he was a mature man, or that he ever "studied" there except in his own close attention to his composition and in the exchange of criticism with such friends as Calvus.[5] He became an interested observer of life in the city, but never mentions the public shows. His contacts ranged from the proconsular dignity of Cicero to Bohemian writers and the fast set of his loved and hated Lesbia.

Though he was possibly a citizen,[6] there is no hint of his having any ambition for a public career, and he shows little sense of politics or history. His antagonism for Caesar, for example, seems to have been triggered by the great man's private behavior and associations rather than by any political question. His change of heart[7] was again a personal matter that perhaps demonstrates the power of Caesar's charm when he chose to exercise it.

Catullus came to regard the Roman city as home and he thus explains to a friend why he cannot send him from Verona the writings he has requested (68.33ff.):

> nam quod scriptorum non magna est copia apud me,
>   hoc fit quod Romae vivimus: illa domus,
> illa mihi sedes, illic mea carpitur aetas;
>   huc una ex multis capsula me sequitur.[a]

Catullus might not have chosen to be preserved for posterity in such a haphazard collection as has come down to us in the one surviving manuscript of his work.[8] The book includes finished poems and fragments, exquisite love poems and coarse invective, elegiac compositions in epigrams and longer pieces, one direct transation from Callimachus, one venture in the difficult galliambic meter, and one epyllion in over four hundred hexameters. Besides what it teaches us of verse technique, which obviously fascinated its writer, the collection gives

---

[a] "for as to there being no great supply of writings ready at hand, this is because I live in Rome: there is my home, there my abiding place, there my days are garnered; hither there comes with me only one out of my many cases of books."

22

us a glimpse of a gifted poet's way of life and work, his use of Latin both colloquial and literary, the range of his reading, his chosen associates. He had no patron and wanted none since he was born to independence. To be sure, he writes to a friend in a witty invitation to dinner (13.7f.) that his purse contains only spider webs:

—nam tui Catulli
plenus sacculus est aranearum.

That cliché was doubtless already old when Plautus used it (*Aul.* 83) and suggests nothing more serious than that he has run through his allowance and cannot, like modern youth, reverse the telephone charges to Verona to ask for an advance. He complains, too (10.9ff.), that he profited not at all from his expedition to Bithynia on the governor's staff, but he traveled home in a yacht built for him (4) and returned to a beautiful villa at Sirmio (31) on Lake Garda. Of this he calls himself *erus* (master) (31.12), though *eri filius* (master's son) might have been more accurate. Not far from the capital he had a country place of his own, which he says the malicious might stigmatize as Sabine, though it was on the fringe of fashionable Tibur (44).

Cicero never names Catullus, though we assume he includes him in his allusions to the younger set of writers. All the terms by which modern writers refer to that group come from Cicero, who seems by the use of general epithets to avoid honoring any one of them by special mention.[9]

Catullus, however, does refer to Cicero directly and indirectly. He addresses to him one little poem of seven hendecasyllables (49) which has been variously interpreted:

Disertissime Romuli nepotum,
quot sunt quotque fuere, Marce Tulli,
quotque post aliis erunt in annis,
gratias tibi maximas Catullus
agit pessimus omnium poeta,   5
tanto pessimus omnium poeta
quanto tu optimus omnium patronus.[b]

Appropriately for the person addressed, there is only one elision, and that of the easiest sort, in the last line. This restraint is notable, because, as G. P. Goold notes, "in the Catullus text we find elision almost a thousand times and in almost every conceivable position."[10]

On the surface these seven lines of 49 are a gracious acknowledgment from a well-bred young man to a distinguished elder for a favor unknown to us. Yet some have read into it a stinging sarcasm in the unexpected closing word and the possible implication that Cicero was ready to defend any applicant, whatever the circumstances, and also in the effect on the balancing clause of the fact that Catullus is far from judging himself a bad poet. The deprecating tone here recalls 1.8f., where he says to Cornelius Nepos:

quare habe tibi quidquid hoc libelli
qualecumque,—[c]

Havelock[11] speaks of "his careless pride and assurance which could normally afford to forget itself in order to charm."

[b] "Most eloquent of the grandsons of Romulus, of all there are and have been, Marcus Tullius, and of all there will be in other years to come, Catullus, the worst poet of all, gives you heartiest thanks, Catullus as much the worst poet of all as you are the best advocate of all."

[c] "so then take for yourself what there is of this book, such as it is."

It is possible to find double meanings in 49, but there have always been scholars to take it for the sincere expression of thanks "suggested by the natural meaning of the words."[12]

Whatever the intention of 49, there can be no question of the malice of another reference, if not to Cicero personally, at least to one of his current publications. This is 84, which concerns the unfortunate speech habits of one Arrius, who misuses his aspirates. Though pronunciation is not the entire burden of the song, it is a theme so dominant that it has distracted readers from other meanings the epigram may carry.[13]

> chommoda dicebat, si quando commoda vellet
>   dicere, et insidias Arrius hinsidias,
> et tum mirifice sperabat se esse locutum
>   cum quantum poterat dixerat hinsidias.
> credo, sic mater, sic liber avunculus eius,   5
>   sic maternus avus dixerat atque avia.
> hoc misso in Syriam requierant omnibus aures:
>   audibant eadem haec leniter et leviter,
> nec sibi postilla metuebant talia verba,
>   cum subito adfertur nuntius horribilis   10
> ionios fluctus, postquam illuc Arrius isset,
>   iam non Ionios esse, sed, Hionios.[d]

[d] "Arrius when he wished to speak of *advantages* would call them *hadvantages*, and *ambushes*, *hambushes*. And then he would hope that he had spoken marvelously well when he had said 'hambushes' with all the force he could muster. I suppose his mother talked in this fashion, and his free uncle, and also his maternal grandfather and grandmother. When he was sent into Syria everybody's ears had a rest; they continued to hear the same things, but lightly and softly spoken, nor did they fear for themselves such words thereafter, when suddenly the dreadful news arrived that the Ionian waves after Arrius had gone that way were no longer Ionian but Hionian."

Here Catullus reverts to more normal use of elision, though only to the number of seven in twelve lines. The studied order of the words allows the metrical stress to fall smartly on every one of the crucial syllables, but so naturally that one might wonder how else the author could have shaped the phrases.

The allusion to the expedition to Syria dates the poem in 55 B.C. when Crassus, the patron of Arrius, assumed the governorship of that province.[14]

Though the verbal resemblance of Catullus 84.5ff. and Cicero, *de oratore* III.45 has of course been noted,[15] nobody seems to have pointed out the essential relation of the epigram to the Ciceronian passage published in the same year.[16] In fact, Ellis in his commentary on Catullus (p. 459) inverts the situation by his astonishing remark, "If Cicero copied Catullus, this epigram must have been known to him in November of 55 B.C." It needs no long study to realize that Catullus is echoing Cicero and not *vice versa*. The poet could not have failed to react with mounting resentment as he read one section of the *de oratore* (III.40-45). The speaker is Lucius Crassus, the orator whom Cicero most admired from the preceding generation, and whom he made the spokesman for his own opinions in *de oratore*. Crassus declares that Rome set the standard for Latin as Athens for Greek (*de oratore* III.42f.):[17] "—hanc dico suavitatem quae exit ex ore: quae quidem ut apud Graecos Atticorum, sic in Latino sermone huius est urbis maxime propria."[e] He goes on to claim that the most illiterate of Athenians or Romans can vanquish the best educated provincials in "lenitate vocis

[e] ". . . I mean actual charm of utterance, a merit which as among the Greeks it is peculiar to Attica, so in Latin speech is specially the attribute of this city." Rackham.

atque ipso oris pressu."[f] He then enters a plea to preserve the precious heritage of Roman speech from provincial corruption (*De Oratore* III.44): "Quae cum sit quaedam certa vox Romani generis urbisque propria, in qua nihil offendi, nihil displicere, nihil animadverti possit, nihil sonare aut olere peregrinum, hanc sequamur, neque solum rusticam asperitatem sed etiam peregrinam insolentiam fugere discamus. (45.) Equidem cum audio socrum meam Laeliam—facilius enim mulieres incorruptam antiquitatem conservant quod multorum sermonis expertes ea tenent semper quae prima didicerunt—sed eam sic audio ut Plautum mihi aut Naevium videar audire: sono ipso vocis ita recto et simplici est ut nihil ostentationis aut imitationis afferre videatur; ex quo sic locutum esse eius patrem iudico, sic maiores, non aspere, ut ille quem dixi, non vaste, non rustice, non hiulce, sed presse ac aequabiliter et leniter."[g]

---

[f] "in smoothness of voice and in actual distinctness of pronunciation and tone."

[g] "Consequently as there is a particular accent peculiar to the Roman race and to our city, involving no possibility of stumbling, or of causing offence, or unpleasantness, or objection, no note or flavour of provincialism, let us make this accent our model, and learn to avoid not only rustic roughness but also provincial solecisms. For my own part when I hear my wife's mother Laelia—since it is easier for women to keep the old pronunciation unspoiled as they do not converse with a number of people and so always retain the accents they heard first— well, I listen to her with the feeling that I am listening to Plautus or Naevius: the actual sound of her voice is so unaffected and natural that she seems to introduce no trace of display or affectation; and I consequently infer that that was how her father and her ancestors used to speak—not harshly, like the person I mentioned, not with a broad or countrified or jerky pronunciation, but neatly and evenly and smoothly." Rackham.

Since Catullus was himself a *peregrinus* from a province, he would naturally resent both Cicero's arrogant assumption of Roman superiority and his dismissal of all outsiders as marked by displeasing speech. The words put into the mouth of Crassus he would feel were insulting not to himself alone, but to the high standing of his family, to the scholars who had been his teachers, to such gifted *conterranei* as Valerius Cato, Cinna, and Varus. He retaliates in 84 with the wit and the power over words that Cicero perhaps underestimated. Catullus had not lived in Rome as a recluse. He had associated with the well-born and prominent, but he had also mingled with the populace in public places. In the courts and in the Forum his sensitive ear had caught and registered for his amusement some local turns of speech that hardly supported Cicero's notion of the *suavitas* prevailing in the utterance of all Romans high and low. In his burlesque of Cicero's praise of Laelia, Catullus has used as her counterpart Quintus Arrius, who seems to be the same as a base-born orator mentioned in the *Brutus* 242. Without talent or training the man had managed by dancing attendance on the influential to acquire some degree of professional success.[18] Arrius had played second fiddle (as *quasi secondarius*) to Marcus Crassus. Though he was "infimo loco natus" (*Brutus* 242), there is no evidence that he was not a Roman.[19] The fact that Catullus chose him for his instrument here is an argument for his being no *peregrinus* but one of Cicero's Romans who could do no linguistic wrong. By contrast with Cicero's grand old lady in her aristocratic setting, he is of low birth. To judge from the mention of relatives on the mother's side only and to the adjective *liber* pointedly applied to the uncle in line 5, the family had risen only recently from servile status.[20] Arrius, like Laelia, has retained the accents he had learned in childhood but what his family had bequeathed to him was a life-long handicap.

> credo, sic mater, sic liber avunculus eius,
> sic maternus avus dixerat atque avia.

These lines are an obvious parallel for Cicero's "sic locutum esse eius patrem iudico, sic maiores,—non aspere, non vaste, non rustice, non hiulce, sed presse et aequabiliter et leniter" (*de oratore* III.45 fin.). Catullus picks up the end of the speech about Laelia with "leniter et leviter" in line 8 of his epigram. A special touch is added by Laelia's connection with Lucius Crassus, Cicero's favorite orator, while Arrius is a hanger-on of Marcus Crassus, the triumvir. Toward the latter Cicero cherished a long-standing antagonism, never fully relinquished in spite of a reconciliation accepted under pressure for the sake of public relations.[21]

It is possible that Cicero never read the Arrius epigram, since he re-used the example of Laelia without embarrassment nine years later in *Brutus* 211: "Auditus est nobis Laeliae C.f. saepe sermo; ergo illam patris elegantia tinctam vidimus."[h]

It is difficult for us to adjust ourselves to the idea that Cicero, as a distinguished orator, author, and statesman, only occasionally glanced across the generation gap to see Catullus as an unimportant young provincial with a misguided absorption in poetry rather than in public matters. Calvus became a force with which he must reckon (*Brutus* 284, 288; *Ad Fam.* xv.21.4), but as an orator not as a poet.[22] The occasional verse of Catullus and his

[h] "More than once I heard Laelia, the daughter of Gaius, conversing and so I realized that her speech was colored by her father's careful usage."

friends had little claim on the attention of a personage over-burdened by political anxieties and frankly acknowledging indifference to lyric poetry in general.[23]

However, if Cicero did not notice the Arrius epigram, others eventually did. Quintilian cites it as famous, "nobile" (1.5.20), though only for the use and abuse of the Latin aspirate in different times.

It would be a dull listener indeed who, after hearing 84, could greet Cicero's praise of Laelia with anything but amusement. But even if Cicero himself felt its full impact, as is unlikely, he could not without making himself ridiculous resent an innocent lampoon on a defect of pronunciation that he himself would heartily condemn.

In this surface innocence with an undercurrent of hostile ridicule there is a reminder of 49, and the irony some have felt beneath its appearance of charming courtesy.

There can be no doubt that, for Catullus, sound is in itself an important means of communication. Elision is only one of many devices by which he shapes the sound to serve his ends. "Far from avoiding elisions he favors them," writes Owen Lee, who observes in this connection that in Catullan usage the elided syllables are "almost certainly" pronounced.[24] D. A. West is also one of those who realize that the numerous elisions of Catullus are not a sign of carelessness or ineptitude but "a resource deliberately exploited."[25] There is convincing evidence of its intentional use in the notorious closing line of 73.

This line has been roundly condemned by generations of scholars,[26] but more and more readers are recognizing it as carefully designed, even though the purpose of the scheme has not been satisfactorily explained.[27]

In its context, 73.6 is all the more striking because it

follows five lines smooth and unbroken except for the negligible *immo etiam* in line 4. After this plain sailing we are hardly prepared for a close that not only shows a sequence of six words cemented together by elision but defies an apparently prevailing rule by bridging with an elision the diaeresis in the pentameter.[28]

> Desine de quoquam quicquam bene velle mereri
>   aut aliquem fieri posse putare pium.
> omnia sunt ingrata, nihil fecisse benigne:
>   immo etiam taedet, taedet obestque magis:
> ut mihi, quem nemo gravius nec acerbius urget   5
>   quam modo qui me unum atque unicum amicum habuit.[i]

If one drops the elided syllables in the climax of line 6 (as the comments plainly show has usually been done), the result is a succession of *K* and *Q* sounds, ugly and meaningless. It is a shock to have Wilkinson, who has written with so much understanding about "expressiveness" in Latin poetry,[29] at this point pose the question: "Is it fanciful to feel a break in the voice, a sobbing effect in the *Q*'s and *K*'s and elisions of Catullus's final pentameter about his faithless friend?" This is indeed a desperate attempt to reconcile the clear meaning of the words with the cacophony produced by reading them in a fashion their author never intended. (Where, by the way, did sobs ever click with *Q* and *K* sounds?)

If, instead of omitting the elided elements, we retain them in accordance with what seems to be the regional

---

[i] "Give up wishing to deserve well of any one or supposing that any one can prove loyal. All is ingratitude, it is nothing to have conferred favors: rather it is a block and a hindrance, as it has been for me whom no one subjects to more bitter and cruel stress than the man who but now held me his one and only friend."

habit in north Italy,[30] the *M* sounds so strongly predomi-
nate that the *Q* and *K* sounds count for nothing. But we
must pause to ask: "How did the Romans pronounce
final *M*'s?" The answer is by no means easy. Soubiran in
his introduction, page 7, calls it an open question, and
later (pp. 131f.) alludes to the confusion and inconsis-
tency of the ancient evidence.[31] Cicero unfortunately
never alludes to the matter. Modern discussions all start
from Quintilian who is somewhat confused himself. The
basic passage in his *Institutes of Oratory* is IX.4.40:
"Atqui eadem illa littera [i.e. *M*] quotiens ultima est et
vocalem verbi sequentis ita contingit ut in eam transire
possit, etiamsi scribitur, tamen parum exprimitur, ut
Multum ille et *Quantum erat*, adeo ut paene cuiusdam
novae litterae sonum reddat. Neque enim eximitur sed
obscuratur et tantum aliqua inter duas vocales velut nota
est, ne ipsae coeant."[j]

Quintilian has evidently found it hard to describe his
final *M* and has borrowed from the visual field a term for
an auditory experience "obscurata." Priscian carries on
the same image in his note on the three possible positions
of *M* in a word.[32] "*M* obscurum in extremitate dictionum
sonat, ut *templum*, apertum in principio, ut *magnus*,
mediocre in mediis, ut *umbra*."[k] The weakness of final

[j] "Moreover that same letter (*M*) whenever it is placed last
and makes contact with a vowel in the following word in such
a way that it might merge with it, even if it is written, it is
sounded very lightly as in *Multum ille* and *Quantum erat*, to a
point where it almost has the sound of some strange letter. For
it is not eliminated but is made less distinct and is like a mark
set between two vowels only to keep them from running
together."

[k] "*M* is indistinct at the end of a word, as in *templum*, open
at the beginning, as in *magnus*, mediocre in the middle, as in
umbra."

M is attested by its frequent omission in some early inscriptions,[33] and by special symbols devised to indicate its difference from *M* in other positions.[34] Most scholars seem to agree with Niedermann's conclusion that final *M* early became a vestigial nasal sound, counting for nothing in itself, but still "making position" for the preceding vowel.[35] This explanation can be completely accepted only if we ignore what Quintilian says in a later passage (XII.10.31): "Quid quod pleraque nos illa quasi mugiente littera cludimus *M*, qua nullum Graece verbum cadit at illi ny iucundum et in fine praecipue quasi tinnientem illius locum ponunt, quae est apud nos rarissima in clausulis."[1] This *M mugiens* can hardly be the same as the *M* Quintilian describes in IX.4.40, the vestigial nasal sound counting for nothing in itself. It is pronounced with closed lips and is scarcely to be distinguished from the *M in principio* and *in mediis* of Priscian's classifications of the final *M*, one the well-attested light nasal in tions of the final *M*, the one the well-attested light nasal in the southern region, where word endings were always less emphasized, and the other in the north, where even elided endings were still pronounced and where the closed sound of the *M mugiens* counted for a great deal.

Before digressing for cases in Lucretius and Virgil, let us return to Catullus 73.6 to see what the *M* sounds mean in that context. Every one of the seven *M*'s in 73.6 is *mugiens*; they represent the letter *M* in all of Priscian's three positions and though those "in extremitate" are the

---

[1] "again, we close a number of words with *M*, a letter which suggests the mooing of a cow, and is never the final letter in any Greek word: for in its place they use the letter *v*, the sound of which is naturally pleasant and produces a ringing tone especially when it comes at the end of a word, whereas in Latin this termination hardly ever occurs."

most important, all work together to build up a remarkable effect. The repetition of the elided, but sounded
M's, with the necessary scanting of their vowels, produces a worrying, mumbling sound which might recall
the promise of 9.8f.:

> —applicansque collum
> iucundum os oculosque saviabor.[m]

There, however, Catullus is greeting a close friend on his
return from a stay abroad. In 73.6 the insincere and
hence loathsome demonstration is cut off by the final
syllable of *habuit*, sharply stressed by its position in the
pentameter and carrying a suggestion of angry violence
in the snap of the *T* at the end. A similar experience is
reflected in a line of Lucilius but the sound there is feeble
and ineffective by comparison: "commanducatur totum
complexu' comestque."[36] Yet even Ferguson,[37] for all his
keenness, has thrown away those priceless elided *M*'s and
arrived at nothing better than "Although we see that the
harshness of the passage deliberately matches the harshness of the sentiment, such a poet would not commend
himself to the elegant Ovid." Properly read, the passage
is not harsh, but soft, though revolting as its writer intended. Catullus has expressed exactly what he meant,
not by a barrage of the strong language we know he had
at his command but by imitating the effect of kisses
mumbled against his cheek until he flings the wretch off
in *habuit*. Far from being "inept" or "technically incom-
petent," 73.6 is a brilliantly successful mimesis of what
the words describe. To do justice to the sound of the
verse indeed requires the *daedala lingua* of a Transpa-

[m] ". . . and bending down your neck, I'll kiss your delightful
mouth and eyes."

34

dane, but we can admire even if we cannot adequately render a sound pattern so skillfully contrived without resort to anything forced or even unusual in the choice or arrangement of the words.

Throughout what we have of his work we find that Catullus has made the most of the letter *M*'s possibilities in all its positions.[38] The same is true of Lucretius and Virgil and, to a less striking extent, Propertius. Though no Transpadane, Propertius as an Umbrian is northern enough to be closer in the sound of his Latin to Catullus than to Tibullus and Ovid. His ear had been trained outside the zone of the nasalized final *M* which Wilkinson[39] feels lessens the "expressiveness" of Propertius 1.20.48, where Hylas is drawn by the nymphs into their spring. But *M mugiens* has its full force when *tum sonitum* is pronounced by a northerner.

How Lucretius can play on the sounds of *M* may be seen for example in his description of the rumbling threats of Mt. Aetna (1.722ff.):

hic est vasta Charybdis et hic Aetnaea minantur
murmura flammarum rursum se colligere iras,
faucibus eruptos iterum vis ut vomat ignis
ad caelumque ferat flammai fulgura rursum.[n]

To translate these lines is to destroy them, because the rolling *R*, the vowels, and the repeated *M mugiens* on which their sound depends all disappear with the Latin words. One has only to read them with the Niedermann nasals to realize how impossible it is to substitute a feeble

[n] "here is devasting Charybdis and here the rumblings of Aetna threaten to gather once more the flames of its wrath, that again in its might it may belch forth the fires bursting from its throat, and once more dash to the sky its flashing flames." Bailey.

grunt for the final *M*'s so necessary for the volcano's rumble.

In *Aeneid* 1.244ff., Virgil makes a similar use of *M* to imitate the booming echo in the rocky channels of Antenor's Timavus:

> regna Liburnorum et fontem superare Timavi,
> unde per ora novem vasto cum murmure montis
> it mare proruptum et pelago premit arva sonanti.º

It seems impossible to think of throwing away the full *M mugiens* in the prodelisions after *Liburnorum* and *proruptum* in lines 244 and 246.

J. P. Elder[40] comments on "the gently insistent recurrence of *um*" in Catullus 34.9-12:

> montium domina ut fores
> silvarumque virentium   10
> saltuumque reconditorum
> amniumque sonantum;ᴾ

Of the ten *M*'s in this strophe, not one can be dismissed as a vestigial sound of no importance in itself. If we do not give the full value of the *M mugiens* to the end of *reconditorum*, though it is hypermetric and elided before *amniumque* in the fourth line, much of the roaring of the mountain stream is silenced, since the subsequent *M* sounds are reinforced by this one. The northern poets exploit the varied possibilities of *M* to imitate the sounds of wind or water, or to express moods, espe-

---

º ". . . realms of the Liburnians and pass the spring of Timavus, whence through nine mouths with a mountain's mighty roar it comes a bursting flood and buries the fields under its sounding sea." Fairclough.

ᴾ "that you might be the mistress of mountains and of the greening woods, of hidden glens and sounding streams."

cially of sorrow;[41] occasionally it suggests pleasure in the taste of food or in the gloating satisfaction Catullus feels in his *lepidum novum libellum* as he turns the roll over in his hands (1.1). The *M*'s moan through 101 and other passages where the poet mourns his dead brother (68.89-100):

> Troia (nefas) commune sepulcrum Asiae Europaeque,
>   Troia virum et virtutum omnium acerba cinis: 90
> quaene etiam nostro letum miserabile fratri
>   attulit. Hei misero frater adempte mihi,
> hei misero fratri iucundum lumen ademptum,
>   tecum una tota est nostra sepulta domus,
> omnia tecum una perierunt gaudia nostra,   95
>   quae tuus in vita dulcis alebat amor.
> Quem nunc tam longe non inter nota sepulcra
>   nec prope cognatos compositum cineres,
> sed Troia obscena, Troia infelice sepultum
>   detinet extremo terra aliena solo.[q]   100

The sad sound of *M* is suspended in line 96 where the joys of old association are recalled, but it recurs thereafter to mark the melancholy remoteness of the burial place so far from home and kindred.

The most poignant reflection of the brother's loss is of course 101, which no one reads and forgets:

[q] "Troy (a curse upon it), the common tomb of Europe and Asia; Troy, the bitter funeral ashes of all heroes and all valour: Troy that has even brought wretched death to my brother! Alas, my brother, torn away from wretched me. Alas, the blessed light of life torn away from my poor brother. With you our whole house lies buried. Together with you have perished all my joys which your sweet love nourished in your life time. You whom now so far away, not among familiar tombs or near the ashes of your kinsmen, but in foul, unfriendly Troy an alien land holds buried in foreign soil."

Multas per gentes et multa per aequora vectus
    advenio has miseras, frater, ad inferias,
ut te postremo donarem munere mortis
    et mutam nequiquam adloquerer cinerem,
quandoquidem fortuna mihi tete abstulit ipsum,   5
    heu miser indigne frater adempte mihi.
Nunc tamen interea haec, prisco quae more parentum
    tradita sunt tristi munere ad inferias,
accipe fraterno multum manantia fletu
    atque in perpetuum, frater, ave atque vale.[r]   10

This had naturally rooted itself in Virgil's mind, and
the echo is unmistakable in the greeting of Anchises to
Aeneas in the lower world (vi.692). However, the re-
union of father and son has a different tone and *M* is no
longer dominant. So "Multas per gentes et multa per
aequora vectus" becomes "quas ego te terras et quanta
per aequora vectum."

Suspension and resumption of elision in Catullus sometimes produce a contrast comparable to that of the coming and going of *M*. Especially effective instances occur
in 76 when the broken expressions of his torment are set
off against words of quiet resolve or acceptance of re-
sponsibility. So the distracted line 11 with its three elisions
is followed by the solid line 12 with none:

[r] "Carried through many nations and across many seas, I
come to these unhappy rites at the tomb, my brother, that I may
give you the last offerings for the dead and speak in vain to your
silent ashes, since fortune has wrested you yourself away from
me, alas, poor brother, wrongfully taken from me! Now, however, meanwhile accept these melancholy funeral offerings
which have been handed down by the ancient custom of our
ancestors and drenched now with a brother's tears, and forever
and ever, my brother, hail and farewell."

quin tu animo offirmas atque istinc teque reducis
    et dis invitis desinis esse miser?[s]

The most resolute line in 76 is number 15 with the hammer strokes of its relentless spondees at the end:

Una salus haec est, hoc est tibi pervincendum;[t]

but his emotion shakes him again and his appeal to the gods in lines 17 to 20 is broken by seven elisions:

O di, si vestrum est misereri, aut si quibus unquam
    extremam iam ipsa in morte tulistis opem,
me miserum adspicite et, si vitam puriter egi,
    eripite hanc pestem perniciemque mihi![u]

Catullus does not use frequent elision anywhere and everywhere but reserves it for places where it can serve some useful purpose. A few short poems (e.g. 41 and 79) have none at all, an arrangement that required careful planning, while other poems (e.g. 42, 46, 48, 49) have no more than one, and that of the easiest sort.

Catullus handles his metrical schemes with the same uncanny skill he shows in his use of elision. The choliambic, at first sight an intractable form, he applies successfully to an astonishing range of subjects. The penultimate foot consists of one augmented long syllable,

---

[s] "why do you not set your mind firmly and bring yourself back from that position and cease to be miserable against the will of the gods?"

[t] "This is the one way of salvation, you must conquer it completely."

[u] "O gods, if it is yours to feel pity, and if you have ever brought help to any at the last moment even at the point of death, look upon me in my misery and if I have lived an upright life, snatch this plague and destruction from me."

heavily stressed, and followed immediately by another stressed element in the last foot. This makes the line stumble at the end and accounts for its name of "the limping iambic." In 8 the halting foot suggests a catch in the throat of the heart-broken lover:

> Miser Catulle, desinas ineptire,
> et quod vides perisse perditum ducas.[v]

But the same meter has a comic effect in 44, where the poet thanks his country house for helping him to cure a cold brought on by the frigid style of a book he found himself forced to read. The halting foot represents a cough or a sneeze at the end of almost half the lines. *Tussis*, the common word for "cough" of course is useful and stands in the final foot of lines 7, 13, and 19, while the sneezes are cleverly imitated by a heavy stress on the syllable *Ti* in lines 1, 5, 11, and 15, and on the first syllable of *frigus* in line 20. While he is being treated "with rest and nettle tea" ("otioque et urtica," line 15) there is one final, emphatic sneeze in *urtica*, but after his cure there are no more symptoms for him, but a cough and a sneeze wished for Sestius who was to blame:

> —quin gravedinem et tussim
> non mi, sed ipsi Sestio ferat frigus,   20
> qui tunc vocat me cum malum librum legi.[w]

In 31, the poem of homecoming to Sirmio, the choliambic is neither sobbing nor comic, but the characteristic break at the line's end is a skip of pure delight, and the

[v] "Wretched Catullus, cease to play the fool and consider lost what you see has perished."
[w] "that the chill style bring a cold and a cough not to me but to Sestius himself who only invites me when I have read his good-for-nothing book."

liveliness of the whole makes it a little dance of joy, culminating in:

ridete, quidquid est domi cachinnorum.[x]   14

A fourth example of the choliambic (22) differs from the three already mentioned. It is quiet and contemplative and is addressed to the future critic, Quintilius Varus, who here in his youth is apparently already known for his taste and judgment. The subject is Suffenus, a would-be poet whom Catullus has cited among bad writers in 14.19. Otherwise charming and polished ("venustus et dicax et urbanus"), Suffenus writes countless good-for-nothing verses which, to make matters worse, he presents in deluxe editions instead of on the scrap paper appropriate to their quality. Since his works have all perished according to their deserts, we cannot be sure, but are tempted to believe that 22 contains some parody of his efforts that Varus would recognize. This would account for the curious roughness of line 4: "Puto esse ego illi milia aut decem aut plura,"[y] which has been almost as harshly treated by modern scholars as 73.6. In sound it is out of key with its context; it is most unlike Catullus in its monotonous series of disyllables; its elisions lack the pointed meaning characteristic of Catullan verse; the awkward use of the correlative *aut—aut* seems to be without parallel.

Two more choliambic poems are devoted to the abuse of an otherwise unknown Spaniard named Egnatius who grins perpetually to display his white teeth. Martial (3.20) echoes Catullus in a choliambic epigram on Caius Rufus, who has the same habit of laughing in and out of season. *Ridet* at the end of Martial's poem probably

[x] "ring out, all the laughter, sounds of home."
[y] "I think he has a thousand or ten thousand or more."

satisfied Martial in suspending the point for the final touch, but it misses the mimesis of *renidet*, which Catullus has used instead (and has repeated four times). Basically, *renidet* means "shine" or "be resplendent"[42] but it has a transferred meaning of "smile" similar to our use of the word "beam" in English. Catullus has a special reason for choosing it here, because to pronounce it one must draw back the lips to expose the teeth and so illustrate what Egnatius was doing with his "beaming" smile:

quod candidos habet dentes.

Perhaps Catullus shows his mastery of sound and rhythm most strikingly in the simplest of his forms, the phalaecean or hendecasyllabic. This is a trochaic measure varied only by a cyclic dactyl in the second foot, and by unlimited license in varying the quantities in the first foot.[43] There is no built-in variety as there is in the strophe forms Horace favors, and to avoid monotony in the repetition of the same scheme throughout the poem is a severe test of the writer's skill. "No other poet of antiquity was skillful enough to discover in so tiny a metre such daring resources."[44] Catullus uses it for an astonishing range of theme and mood, for light occasional verse (13), for love poems to Lesbia (5 and 7), for animated anecdote (10), for a rollicking drinking song (27), for a self-pitying bid for sympathy (38), for a happy spring song (46) with much the same feeling as the choliambics of 31, for coarse invective (16), for the expression of affection for a friend (9). He can make it merry or sad, caustic or loving, ribald or circumspect as he chooses. He varies it sometimes by artful elision, sometimes simply by words of contrasting length and carefully spaced word breaks (5.4-6).

Soles occidere et redire possunt:
nobis, cum semel occidit brevis lux,
nox est perpetua una dormienda.ᶻ

The position of the abrupt *lux* emphasizes the shortness
of the day vouchsafed us, while the oblivion that follows
goes on forever in the beautiful lingering sound of *dormienda*. We can feel the angry jerk of his head as he
reverts to the *vivamus* of the beginning with the abrupt
demand, "Da mi basia mille." *Da* after *dormienda* has
almost the force of a blow. To appreciate the pattern one
has only to compare Horace's *Odes* 1.28.15f., which
treats the same familiar theme of inevitable death, but
which succeeds rather in spite of sound and rhythm than
because of them. Here it is the endless night that the poet
clips short by his final monosyllable:

> —sed omnes una manet nox
> et calcanda semel via leti.ᵃᵃ

In 3, on the death of Lesbia's sparrow, the poor little
bird goes down the road to Hades sad and lonely. He
starts (line 11) in monosyllables, hop, hop, hop, hop, "qui
nunc it per," then picks up a little more impetus in two
hops of *iter*, and now being really under way he moves
decidedly through the five continuous hops of *tenebricosum*:

> qui nunc it per iter tenebricosum.ᵇᵇ

ᶻ "Suns may set and rise again for us; when once our brief day
has finished there is one everlasting night to be slept through."
ᵃᵃ "One night awaits everybody and the road of death must
be trodden."
ᵇᵇ "who now goes along the shadowy road."

43

Finally on his dignity as a full-fledged shade, he proceeds through the fine, mock-heroic:

illuc unde negant redire quemquam.^{cc}

no longer hopping, but apparently *striding*.

Here we have a demonstration of the effect of word breaks that carry a kind of rhythm of their own apart from the metrical pattern. Quintilian, though speaking of prose (IX.4.98) seems to refer to this factor: "Est enim quoddam ipsa divisione verborum latens tempus."^{dd}

A point to notice is that Catullus has used *tenebricosum* in 3.11 instead of the more usual *tenebrosum* because it gives him an invaluable extra syllable. *Basiationes* in 7.1 is a similar case where he has chosen the long form in place of *basia*. Such polysyllables have been criticized as old-fashioned and clumsy but are a saving grace in the hendecasyllables where they might be compared to the timber courses in a mud-brick wall—long, continuous binders to hold the small blocks together. Without them the lines might be both choppy and monotonous. Catullus has skillfully avoided the creation of another sort of monotony by placing his words of five or six or even seven syllables in different positions in the lines. In "Quaeres quot mihi basiationes" (7.1) we find the long word at the end; in line 4 of the same poem *laserpiciferis* is at the beginning; in line 11 *pernumerare* is in the middle.

Catullus has left only one drinking song of seven hendecasyllables (27). There was no need of another.

^{cc} "to that place whence they say no one returns."
^{dd} "For there is in the very division of words a hidden rhythm."

Minister vetuli puer Falerni
inger mi calices amariores,
ut lex Postumiae iubet magistrae,
ebrioso acino ebriosioris.
At vos quo libet hinc abite, lymphae,   5
vini pernicies, et ad severos
migrate: hic merus est Thyonianus.ᵉᵉ

Surely the *latens tempus* of the word breaks here is
beyond praise, especially in the reel and sway of the
fourth line, with its artful elision. The sudden jerk of the
hiccup in *hic* of the last line is thrown into high relief by
the soft elision just before it, an uninhibited touch Cicero
might have found offensive. In fact, if Cicero had ever
mentioned Catullus (as he never did), what he had to
say of him would probably have been like the last message to Lesbia: "non bona dicta."

ᵉᵉ "Young cup-bearer of old Falernian wine, bring me more
pungent cups as bids the rule of our toast-mistress, Postumia,
more drunken than the drunken grape. But to whatever place
you wish, get hence, water, the bane of wine, and travel to the
sober: here is pure Bacchus."

III

Lucretius: Northern Linguistics

Of all the great names in Latin literature, that of
Lucretius is the most obscure. We know far less
about him than about Catullus, who has largely compen-
sated for the lack of an ancient biography by what he has
told us of himself in his poems.[1] On the other hand, the
only work we possess from Lucretius is the poorest
possible vehicle for such revelations, a great didactic
poem on the Epicurean system. There can be no doubt
that for years before he composed the *De Rerum Natura*
Lucretius had been writing verse and studying verse
technique, but all his earlier efforts are lost to us. In-
evitably the existence of a greatly gifted writer, about
whom his own generation has given us practically no
information, inspired inventions to give him a background once his work became known. Suetonius, a
century and a half after the poet's death, would find
material if he decided to include him in the *De Viris
Illustribus*.

It seems futile to rehearse once more the conflicting
conjectures scholars have based on the woefully meager
and unreliable tradition about Lucretius. It has all been
ably and completely presented in easily accessible commentaries and editions of the poet.[2] But after all the argument and interpretation, we are left with nothing reason-
ably certain except that Titus Lucretius Carus was born
in the opening years of the first century B.C. and died at
the age of forty-four in 55 B.C. or shortly thereafter. His

46

birthplace is nowhere recorded. His life overlapped that of Catullus, but he was fourteen or fifteen years older. A slightly more archaic color in his language may be partly a result of this time difference, and partly due to his never having adopted the capital as his home. One instance of more archaic usage is in the suppression of final *S* before consonants, an old-fashioned practice that occurs quite frequently in Lucretius but only once in Catullus.[3] Cornelius Nepos implies by his reference to the two poets (in his life of Atticus 12.4) that they died at approximately the same time. We know from their mutual borrowings that there was some contact between them, but neither mentions the other by name.

There are no contemporary references to Lucretius except one sentence in a letter from Cicero to his brother Quintus (*Ad Q. Fr.* ii.10[9].3), and the passage from Nepos cited above.

The differences between Catullus and Lucretius are so striking that scholars have tended to disregard the resemblances, though they constitute the best evidence we possess on the place of Lucretius's origin. Sikes[4] goes so far as to say that they have nothing in common except the epoch in which they both lived. This is a great exaggeration, but it reflects the contrast readers have felt between them. Catullus is an intensely personal poet, interested in himself and in the individual friends and foes who affected his life. Lucretius is possessed by a missionary's zeal to rescue mankind from the burden of superstition and particularly from the fear of death. He hardly intrudes his own personality into the work except to declare his aim and to express his idolatrous admiration for Epicurus, whose teachings provide the means of accomplishing that aim.[5] Though his great theme is so remote from Catullan subjects, in his handling of the language he is closely akin to Catullus and opposed to Cicero. The most obvious, though by no means the only, bond with Catullus is in his use of elision, those open vowel junctions to which Cicero applies such epithets as *rusticus* and *peregrinus* to mark them as alien to the *urbanitas* of the capital.[6] Like Catullus, Lucretius fails to meet the standards championed by Cicero as characteristic of Roman speech and superior to those of any other locality. Indeed he is so far from conforming to them that it is hard to understand how the theory that Lucretius was a Roman born and bred ever gained such wide acceptance. The similarity not only of their elision usage[7] but of their sound effects in general strongly suggests that Catullus and Lucretius had heard the same regional speech from their earliest days and from common experience had acquired the same delicately tuned ear, the same nimble tongue, and the same use of sound as a practical means of communication. Their difference from Cicero is enough to show that their resemblance to each other is not to be explained solely by the fact that they are both late Republicans.

Lucretius, like Catullus, uses or suppresses elision to produce intentional effects and intends the elided syllables to be fully pronounced,[8] though in clipped time to avoid destroying the dominant beat of the verse. This retention of elided syllables of course includes those closing in *M*, a question that has already been discussed in Chapter II (pp. 32f.). There it was noted that final *M* is an important sound for Lucretius as for Catullus and Virgil. Lucretius used it (by no means as a "weak vestigial sound")[9] sometimes heavily reinforced by *M*'s in other positions in the words. The letter occurs no less than seven times, for instance, in III.888:

nam si in morte malumst malis morsuque ferarum
tractari

and they all contribute to the unpleasant picture of a
beast gnawing and mauling a body; five of the seven are
not final but initial or medial. Only one *M* survives in
Bailey's version:

for if it be an evil in death to be mauled by the jaws and
teeth of a wild beast,

a good illustration of how easily the original effect can
be destroyed by translation into words of the same
meaning, but with none of the original sound.

For Lucretius as for Catullus, the *M*, elided or not,
carries the full force of Quintilian's *M mugiens* and always supplements the meaning in some way.[10] It may
imitate natural sound, as in the volcanic rumblings of
Aetna (1.722ff.; Chapter II, 35), or the equally natural
sounds associated with the chewing and savoring of
food (IV.618f.):

Principio sucum sentimus in ore, cibum cum
mandendo exprimimus.[a]

This recalls the invitation in Catullus 13:

Cenabis bene, mi Fabulle, apud me
paucis, si tibi di favent, diebus,
si tecum attuleris bonam[11] atque magnam
cenam, . . . [b]

---

[a] "First of all we perceive taste in our mouth when we press it
out in chewing." Bailey.

[b] "You will dine well, my dear Fabullus, at my house in a few
days if the gods are good to you, if you bring with you a fine
big dinner."

where there is a similar "yumyum" effect in the repeated
M, and also the equally vivid mimesis of mouth sounds
of another sort in Catullus 73.6.

The Iphianessa episode of Lucretius 1.84ff. is peculiar
in that not one of the thirty-six *M*'s that fill the lines with
compassion for the young victim happens to be elided:

Aulide quo pacto Triviai virginis aram
Iphianassai turparunt sanguine foede   85
ductores Danaum delecti, prima virorum.
cui simul infula virgineos circumdata comptus
ex utraque pari malarum parte profusast,
et maestum simul ante aras adstare parentem
sensit et hunc propter ferrum celare ministros   90
aspectuque suo lacrimas effundere civis,
muta metu terram genibus summissa petebat.
nec miseras prodesse in tali tempore quibat
quod patrio princeps donarat nomine regem.
nam sublata virum manibus tremibundaque ad aras   95
deductast, non ut sollemni more sacrorum
perfecto posset claro comitari Hymenaeo,
sed casta inceste nubendi tempore in ipso
hostia concideret mactatu maesta parentis,
exitus ut classi felix faustusque daretur.   100
tantum religio potuit suadere malorum.[e]

[e] "Even as at Aulis the chosen chieftains of the Danai, the first
of all the host, foully stained with the blood of Iphianassa the
altar of the Virgin of the Cross-Roads. For as soon as the band
braided about her virgin locks streamed from her either cheek
in equal lengths, as soon as she saw her sorrowing sire stand at
the altar's side, and near him the attendants hiding their knives,
and her countrymen shedding tears at the sight of her, tongue-
tied with terror, sinking on her knees she fell to earth. Nor
could it avail the luckless maid at such a time that she first had
given the name of father to the king. For seized by men's hands,
all trembling was she led to the altars, not that, when the

The *M*'s carry on, however, until in line 101 the feeling shifts to angry sarcasm toward her destroyers, and the *M*'s disappear in:

exitus ut classi felix faustusque daretur.

M sets the prevailing mood of mourning or complaint in the splendid close of Book III (830-1094). It plays an important part in the lament of kinsmen around the bier of the deceased (894-901) and especially in 897ff.:

"non poteris factis florentibus esse tuisque
praesidium. misero misera," aiunt, "omnia ademit
una dies infesta tibi tot praemia vitae."[d]

This is followed by 900:

illud in his rebus non addunt, "nec tibi earum
iam desiderium rerum super insidet una."[e]

Except for *earum* at the end, the *M*'s have dropped out of line 900 as in general they disappear from those remarks that rebuke man for his unreasonable complaints. So when *Natura Rerum* utters a voice, her reprimand in 932ff., after a passage thickly set with *M*'s shows very few. Occasional lines without *M* appear in the midst of

---

ancient rite of sacrifice was fulfilled, she might be escorted by the clear cry of 'Hymen', but in the very moment of marriage, a pure victim she might foully fall beneath a father's slaughtering stroke in sorrow herself, that a happy and hallowed starting might be granted to the fleet. Such evil deeds could religion prompt." Bailey.

[d] " 'you will not be able to prosper in your affairs or to be a defense to your people, miserable as you are,' men say, 'one baneful day has miserably wrested from you all the many boons of life.' "

[e] "in this connection they do not add, 'nor does there survive in you any desire for these things.' "

long passages where *M* dominates, as for instance, line 877:

nec radicitus e vita se tollit et eicit.[f]

Four such lines (1076, 1081, 1086, and 1090) occur at almost exactly regular intervals in the concluding lines of the book (1075-1094). The contrast of sound is striking enough to suggest an intentional pattern such as occurs in the use and suppression of elision throughout the work.

Lucretius's application of elision covers a wide range. Sometimes the broken sound strongly reinforces the meaning, and elsewhere it simply prevents too monotonous a regularity in the movement of the hexameter. The latter purpose is especially evident in the opening lines of the first book. Here the elisions, few in number and all of the easiest description, move back and forth in the lines so that the little ripple they introduce into the rhythm does not itself become monotonous.[12]

> AENEADVM genetrix, hominum divumque voluptas,
> alma Venus, caeli subter labentia signa
> quae mare navigerum, quae terras frugiferentis
> concelebras, per te quoniam genus omne animantum
> concipitur visitque exortum lumina solis: 5
> te, dea, te fugiunt venti, te nubila caeli
> adventumque tuum, tibi suavis daedala tellus
> summittit flores, tibi rident aequora ponti
> placatumque nitet diffuso lumine caelum.
> nam simul ac species patefactast verna diei   10
> et reserata viget genitabilis aura favoni,
> aeriae primum volucres te, diva, tuumque
> significant initum perculsae corda tua vi.

[f] "nor does he remove and cast himself root and branch out of life."

inde ferae pecudes persultant pabula laeta   [15]
et rapidos tranant amnis: ita capta lepore   15 [14]
te sequitur cupide quo quamque inducere pergis.
denique per maria ac montis fluviosque rapacis
frondiferasque domos avium camposque virentis
omnibus incutiens blandum per pectora amorem
efficis ut cupide generatim saecla propagent.   20
quae quoniam rerum naturam sola gubernas
nec sine te quicquam dias in luminis oras
exoritur neque fit laetum neque amabile quicquam,
te sociam studeo scribendis versibus esse
quos ego de rerum natura pangere conor   25
Memmiadae nostro, quem tu, dea, tempore in omni
omnibus ornatum voluisti excellere rebus.
quo magis aeternum da dictis, diva, leporem.
effice ut interea fera moenera militiai
per maria ac terras omnis sopita quiescant.[g]   30

[g] "Mother of Aeneas's line, life-giving Venus, delight of men and gods, who beneath the gliding constellations of the sky throngs the shipbearing sea and the fruitful earth, since through thee every breed of living creatures is conceived, and on coming forth beholds the light of the sun: it is thou, goddess, thou that the winds flee and the clouds of the sky at thy coming; for thee the clever earth puts forth her sweet flowers; for thee the levels of the ocean smile and the sky, its anger spent, shines with radiant light. For as soon as the springtime aspect of the day is revealed and the fertile breeze of Favonius blows strong in renewed freedom, first the birds of the air, deeply smitten by thy power, give token, goddess, of thee and thy coming. Then the wild herds bound over the rich pastures and swim the swift rivers, so captured by delight does each one follow eagerly wherever thou goest on to lead. Then through seas and mountains and tearing rivers, and the leafy homes of birds and green fields, thou strikest beguiling love into the hearts of all and makest them eagerly renew the generations after their kind. Since thou alone dost govern the nature of things and without

53

Lucretius and the Transpadanes

Here we have only easy elision, and in spite of the artful placing of the breaks we are on the verge of being made "faint with too much sweet" when the flick of the monosyllable *vi* at the end of line 13 works with *perculsae* to counteract the softness. *Perculsae*, as has been observed,[13] suggests physical impact as though from a goad. Bailey's "thrilled" hardly suffices to express its force.

Elision is far from being the only device at the disposal of the poet to achieve variety. Line 20 explains by its uninterrupted flow the comparative flutter in the preceding four verses that describe the unrest caused by the touch of Venus on all living creatures.

Elision becomes more frequent in lines 14 to 48, but still shows none of the difficulty that many critics regard as typically Lucretian. We might indeed find here the "soft vocalism" or "sweetness and sensuousness of poetical effect" that Hendrickson thought marked the "graecizing" style of Catullus as contrasted with true Italian vigor.[14] Catullus and Lucretius write lines harmoniously lyrical when they so choose, but use a harsh—or even cacophonous—arrangement when it seems to them expressive of the sentiment or the idea to be communicated. Out of context, a number of passages in the *De Rerum Natura* show enough of such roughness to provoke the sort of condemnation heaped on Catullus 73.6. Duff names "the deformity of clumsy elision" as a conspicuous

thee nothing comes forth into the divine realms of light, or becomes joyous and lovely, I am eager that thou be my helper in writing these verses which I am attempting to compose about the nature of things for our son of the Memmii whom thou, goddess, hast wished at all times to be preeminent and adorned with every grace. So all the more, goddess, give lasting charm to my words. Meanwhile make the fierce works of war subside in peace for all seas and lands."

fault of Lucretian verse.[15] It is quite true that in his extended and complex exposition, the reasons for some of his metrical patterns are not immediately obvious to us, but most of the passages singled out as most disfiguring show that their form was carefully planned and not the result of carelessness or lack of control of verse structure. Stanley B. Smith cites six instances of "awkward or excessive" elision,[16] but these are less harsh and ugly when they are considered in their relation to the context and not excerpted as single lines. Let us take Book IV.741 as an example:

> verum ubi equi atque hominis casu convenit imago.

When the statistically minded remark that here we have four elisions in one line, they understate the case because there are four elisions crowded into one part of the line, as in Catullus 73.6. Nothing could be more solid and direct than the conclusion of this verse in *casu convenit imago*. The passage in which the verse stands describes the merging of the images of horse and man to form that of the monstrous centaur. We are able to conceive such a hybrid, though no image could reach us from a living specimen, because separate images from a man and a horse, so fine and delicate that the poet compares them to gold foil or spider webs (line 727), might cling on contact as they float through the air and so fuse into one monstrous combination before penetrating to our minds. Munro[17] had the wit to comment, "it strikes me that Lucretius here meant the tangled sound to recall the entangling of the incongruous images," but he does not mention in support of his interpretation that the verse in question (IV.741), with its unusual quota of four elisions, is thrown into high relief by the otherwise easy flow of the passage in which it is embedded[18] (724 to 748), where

no line shows more than one easy elision and some have
none at all.

principio hoc dico rerum simulacra vagari
multa modis multis in cunctas undique partis   725
tenvia, quae facile inter se iunguntur in auris,
obvia cum veniunt, ut aranea bratteaque auri.
quippe etenim multo magis haec sunt tenvia textu
quam quae percipiunt oculos visumque lacessunt,
corporis haec quoniam penetrant per rara cientque   730
tenvem animi naturam intus sensumque lacessunt.
Centauros itaque et Scyllarum membra videmus
Cerbereasque canum facies simulacraque eorum
quorum morte obita tellus amplectitur ossa;
omne genus quoniam passim simulacra feruntur,   735
partim sponte sua quae fiunt aere in ipso,
partim quae variis ab rebus cumque recedunt
et quae confiunt ex horum facta figuris.
nam certe ex vivo Centauri non fit imago,
nulla fuit quoniam talis natura animantis,   740
verum ubi equi atque hominis casu convenit imago,
haerescit facile extemplo, quod diximus ante,
propter subtilem naturam et tenvia texta.
cetera de genere hoc eadem ratione creantur.
quae cum mobiliter summa levitate feruntur,   745
ut prius ostendi, facile uno commovet ictu
quaelibet una animum nobis subtilis imago;
tenvis enim mens est et mire mobilis ipsa.[h]

[h] "First of all I say this, that many idols of things wander
about in many ways in all directions on every side, fine idols
which easily become linked with one another in the air, when
they come across one another's path, like spider's web and
gold leaf. For indeed those idols are far finer in their texture
than those which fill the eyes and arouse sight, since these
pierce through the pores of the body, and awake the fine nature

It is the common practice of Lucretius to set his rough or difficult lines in a sequence elided lightly if at all, just as we observed in Catullus 73 that five unusually smooth verses lead up to the difficult close. So when Lucretius argues that *animi natura* can not exist apart from body, the line describing their entanglement (III,793), with its four elisions, stands as if to point the contrast between two unelided lines:

> certum ac dispositumst ubi quicquid crescat et insit.
> sic animi natura nequit sine corpore oriri
> sola neque a nervis et sanguine longius esse.
> quod si posset enim, multo prius ipsa animi vis   790
> in capite aut umeris aut imis calcibus esse
> posset et innasci quavis in parte soleret,
> tandem in eodem homine atque in eodem vase manere.
> quod quoniam nostro quoque constat corpore certum
> dispositumque videtur ubi esse et crescere possit   795
> sorsum anima atque animus, tanto magis infitiandum
> totum posse extra corpus durare genique.[i]

---

of the mind within, and arouse its sensation. And so we see Centaurs and the limbs of Scyllas, and the dog faces of Cerberus, and idols of those who have met death and whose bones are held in the embrace of earth, since idols of every kind are borne everywhere, some which are created of their own accord even in the air, some which depart in each case from divers things, and those again which are made and put together from the shapes of these. For in truth the image of the Centaur comes not from a living thing, since there never was the nature of such a living creature but when by chance the images of man and horse have met, they cling together readily at once as we have said before, because of their subtle nature and fabric. All other things of this kind are fashioned in the same way. And when they move nimbly with exceeding lightness, as I have shown ere now, any one such subtle image stirs our mind; for the mind is fine and of itself wondrous nimble." Bailey.

[i] "It is determined and ordained where each thing can grow

57

Another place on the critics' blacklist is Lucretius 1.337, which occurs in the demonstration that *inane* ("empty space" or "void") must exist with matter throughout the universe, "namque est in rebus inane," as stated in line 330. Otherwise any motion or change would be impossible (lines 335ff.):

> Nec tamen undique corporea stipata tenentur
> omnia natura; namque est in rebus inane.   330
> quod tibi cognosse in multis erit utile rebus
> nec sinet errantem dubitare et quaerere semper
> de summa rerum et nostris diffidere dictis.
> quapropter locus est intactus inane vacansque.
> quod si non esset, nulla ratione moveri   335
> res possent; namque officium quod corporis exstat,
> officere atque obstare, id in omni tempore adesset
> omnibus; haud igitur quicquam procedere posset,
> principium quoniam cedendi nulla daret res.
> at nunc per maria ac terras sublimaque caeli   340
> multa modis multis varia ratione moveri
> cernimus ante oculos, quae, si non esset inane,
> non tam sollicito motu privata carerent
> quam genita omnino nulla ratione fuissent,
> undique materies quoniam stipata quiesset.[j]   345

---

and have its place. So the nature of the mind cannot come to birth alone without body, nor exist far apart from sinews and blood. But if this could be, far sooner might the force of mind itself exist in head or shoulders, or right down in the heels, and be wont to be born in any part you will, but at least remain in the same man and the same vessel. But since even within our body it is determined and seen to be ordained where soul and mind can dwell apart and grow, all the more must we deny that it could continue or be begotten outside the whole body." Bailey.

[j] "And yet all things are not held close pressed on every side

58

Here the elisions of line 337 effectively represent the interlocking or mutual interference that could block all movement of the atoms if they were packed solidly together without the interposition of some empty space. The tangling and stumbling of line 337 contrast with the easy pace of lines 334 to 336, and still more with the two completely unelided verses (338 and 339) which follow immediately with their clear statement of the result of the absence of *inane*.

One of the strongest stylistic bonds with Catullus lies in this suspension and resumption of elision by which the two poets often help to point their meaning. *De Rerum Natura* shows on a grand scale the pattern we find in miniature, so to speak, in Catullus 76, where there is a contrast (undoubtedly carefully designed) between the broken expression of the poet's trouble and the unelided statement of his firm resolve.[19] D. A. West cites another illustration of the scheme in Catullus 68.89ff., where five elisions occur within two lines after thirty-one verses with a total of only nine such breaks. The contrast in the

by the nature of body; for there is void in things. To have learnt this will be of profit to you in dealing with many things; it will save you from wandering in doubt and always questioning about the sum of things, and distrusting my words. There is then a void, mere space untouchable and empty. For if there were not, by no means could things move; for that which is the office of body, to offend and hinder, would at every moment beset all things; nothing, therefore, could advance, since nothing could make a start of yielding place. But as it is, through seas and lands and the high tracts of heaven, we descry many things by many means moving in diverse ways before our eyes, which, if there were not void, would not so much be robbed and baulked of restless motion, but rather could in no way have been born at all; since matter would on every side be in close-packed stillness." Bailey.

frequency of elision marks a transition from "the declamatory poetry of mythology to the plain poetry of personal sorrow."[20]

At the beginning of Lucretius VI, after the doubts, hesitations, and needless turmoil of men's minds have been set forth in the heavily elided sequence of lines 9 to 16, Epicurus diagnoses the troubles of mortals (17-25), and as his healing message takes control of the situation the elisions disappear with the confusion:

> veridicis igitur purgavit pectora dictis.[k]

The elisions do not begin again for eleven lines until in line 35 we come to the picture of children fearful of imaginary terrors in the dark:

> nam veluti pueri trepidant atque omnia caecis
> in tenebris metuunt, . . .[l]

This passage recalls a place in the third book (11-30) where Lucretius expresses a somewhat more personal reaction to the master's revelation of the truth that frees the world from its fears. In lines 11-21 there is a single negligible elision in line 21:

> semperque innubilus aether.[m]

As in VI.24ff., this passage concerns the message of Epicurus, which the poet evidently feels should be conveyed in phrases as firm and direct as possible. The elisions become more numerous when the writer turns from Epicurus to the dark troubles of misguided men who are not living in accordance with his doctrine (31ff.).

---

[k] "with his discourse of truthful words he purged their hearts."
[l] "for even as children tremble and fear everything in blinding darkness. . . ." Bailey.
[m] "an ever cloudless heaven."

Lucretius pauses periodically at the end of a long illustration or a section of his argument for a summary in one terse sentence that he wishes his reader to remember. So at the close of the Iphianassa episode we have in 1.101:

Tantum religio potuit suadere malorum.[n]

It would be possible to build up a synopsis of the system he is advocating by excerpting a series of such *dicta*. The statements, though sometimes couplets, are as a rule ingeniously reduced to a single complete line, are impossible to misunderstand, and are cast in a strong forcible rhythm without noticeable elisions.

The first of these basic precepts in its complete form stands in line 205 of the first book:

nil igitur fieri de nilo posse fatendumst,[o]

but Lucretius has led up to it very carefully through several stages, and presents it as nature's fundamental truth. He precedes it with six clear, unelided lines (140-45) addressed to the individual to whom the entire work is dedicated, and declares the author's happy absorption in his difficult task. In line 146 we come back to the elisions by which Lucretius sometimes seems to prod and jostle us into paying attention. In line 150 stands nature's *principium*, the truth that is to be demonstrated, that nothing is ever produced from nothing by the power of the gods.

sed tua me virtus tamen et sperata voluptas	140
suavis amicitiae quemvis efferre laborem	
suadet et inducit noctes vigilare serenas	
quaerentem dictis quibus et quo carmine demum	

[n] "such evil deeds could religion prompt." Bailey.
[o] "it must be acknowledged then that nothing can be created out of nothing." Bailey.

clara tuae possim praepandere lumina menti,
res quibus occultas penitus convisere possis.   145
    Hunc igitur terrorem animi tenebrasque necessest
non radii solis neque lucida tela diei
discutiant, sed naturae species ratioque
principium cuius hinc nobis exordia sumet,
nullam rem e nilo gigni divinitus umquam.ᵖ   150

As if to serve notice that this is not his final pronounce-
ment, the poet has elided one monosyllable before another
in line 150. Both of these elements, as essential to the
meaning, must be pronounced. After this striking elision
of *rem e* the precept next appears divided between two
lines in 155f.:

quas ob res ubi viderimus nil posse creari
de nilo.�q

Finally, after a series of examples to prove that everything must be produced from its own seed and substance,
the precept is repeated in the one solid line already cited:

nil igitur fieri de nilo posse fatendumst.[21] ʳ

ᵖ "yet your merit and the pleasure of your sweet friendship,
for which I hope, urge me to bear the burden of any toil, and
lead me on to watch through the calm nights, searching by
what words, yea and in what measures, I may avail to spread
before your mind a bright light, whereby you may see to the
heart of hidden things.
    "This terror then of the mind, this darkness must needs be
scattered not by the rays of the sun and the gleaming shafts of
day, but by the outer view and the inner law of nature; whose
first rule shall take its start for us from this, that nothing is ever
begotten of nothing by divine will." Bailey.
    �q "therefore, when we have seen that nothing can be created
out of nothing. . . ." Bailey.
    ʳ "it must be acknowledged then that nothing can be created
out of nothing."

Fatendumst leaves us no choice: at this stage of the argument we must admit that no power in the universe can create something out of nothing. As nothing comes from nothing, nothing is ever utterly destroyed. After an elided sequence in which created things are broken up into their immortal first beginning, we come to three unelided lines (235-237) that conclude that existence continues through the recycling of the components into new forms:

> haud igitur possunt ad nilum quaeque reverti.[8]   237

So the pattern goes on with the alternation of elided process and unelided result made clear by the rhythmical contrast.[22]

For both Catullus and Lucretius the sound of a word, the actual noise it makes when pronounced as well as the motion involved in the act of utterance, has a peculiar importance.

The point has already been raised with Catullus's use of *renidet* rather than *ridet* for the grin of Egnatius,[23] but as in that case Martial failed properly to appreciate the choice, so Aulus Gellius (10.21.9) seems unaware of the essential relation of *radit-gradiens-raditur* in Lucretius iv.528ff. In *radit* the writer has a word of abrasion, of rubbing against, which in its various uses covers a wide range in the degree of violence involved. In v.258 Lucretius uses it of streams eroding their banks and in v.1267 for planing smooth planks from rough timbers, "levia radere tigna," but here in Book iv for the voice rasping its way out of the throat:

> praeterea radit vox fauces saepe facitque   528
> asperiora foras gradiens arteria clamor.[t]

---

[8] "all things cannot then be turned to naught." Bailey.

[t] "moreover, the voice often scrapes the throat and shouting makes the windpipe over-rough as it issues forth." Bailey.

63

Since he obviously feels *radit* the right word for the passage, he repeats it in "ianua raditur oris" (532).[24] In *gradiens* he has found a verb of motion that not only chimes with *radit* and *raditur* but adds another touch of roughness in the hard initial *G*.

So, too, in describing the production of speech sounds by lips and tongue (IV.549-552), he repeats *formatura* (552 and 556), a word he may indeed have invented for his own special use here,[25] since the ordinary word *formatio*, even if it were better adapted for the hexameter, would only flatten out the face of the speaker. In pronouncing *formatura* on the other hand one must act out the whole process it describes: the lips blow out the initial *F*, protrude for the *O*, close for the *M*, protrude again for the *U*, while the tongue snaps the *T* and trills the *R*'s.

> Hasce igitur penitus voces cum corpore nostro
> exprimimus rectoque foras emittimus ore,   550 [548]
> mobilis articulat verborum daedala lingua   [549]
> formaturaque labrorum pro parte figurat.   [550]
> hoc ubi non longum spatiumst unde illa profecta
> perveniat vox quaeque, necessest verba quoque ipsa
> plane exaudiri discernique articulatim.   555
> servat enim formaturam servatque figuram.[u]

It must be noted, however, that the remarkable aptness of the word Lucretius chooses sometimes has little or

[u] "These voices then, when we force them forth from deep within our body, and shoot them abroad straight through our mouth, the pliant tongue, artificer of words, severs apart, and the shaping of the lips in its turn gives them form. Therefore when it is no long distance from which each of those utterances starts, and reaches to us, it must needs be that the very words too are clearly heard and distinguished sound by sound. For each utterance preserves its shaping and preserves its form." Bailey.

nothing to do with sound or motion or a combination of the two. It may be a question of meaning only and may depend on its application being unusual enough to give it a lively force in its context. This is the case with a Greek word *nothus*,[26] which both Lucretius and Catullus apply picturesquely to the light of the moon. Its basic meaning is apparently "illegitimate," "born out of wedlock," and it is most naturally associated with men or with cross-bred animals (as in Virgil's *Aeneid* IX.697 and VII.283), but various transferred meanings also occur.[27] In the present instance the moon shows as her own a radiance "not genuine" but reflected from another luminous body. This is a clear case of borrowing between Catullus and Lucretius. In some obviously related passages it is impossible to say which poet drew from the other, but here in Book V it is plain that Lucretius was first with

> lunaque sive notho fertur loca lumine lustrans   575
> sive suam proprio iactat de corpore lucem.[v]

Catullus has made a choice between the alternatives Lucretius offers, and has reduced the exaggerated alliteration of the original:

> et notho es   34.15
> dicta lumine luna.[w]

Catullus was likewise the follower in his first marriage song where the torches' flames flaring back in the wind are presented as shining locks tossed back from a young brow:

[v] "the moon too, whether she illumines places with a borrowed light as she moves along, or throws out her own rays from her own body." Bailey.

[w] "or art called luna from thy borrowed light."

Viden ut faces   61.77
splendidas quatiunt comas?[x]

The image is Catullus's own, but surely he was remembering the cadences in several passages where Lucretius describes shooting stars as the torches of the night sky trailing brightness behind them:

nocturnasque faces caeli sublime volantis   II.206
nonne vides longos flammarum ducere tractus
in quascumque dedit partis natura meatum?[y]

tempore nocturno, tum splendida signa videntur[z] IV.444

noctivagaeque faces caeli flammaeque volantes[aa] V.1191

Infinity opens beneath our feet in the tiny puddle that reflects the sky, the finger-deep puddle Lucretius designates in a characteristically vivid expression "collectus aquae" (IV.414). The name gives us the whole process of its formation by trickles that "gather" in the little hollow where three stones meet:[28]

at collectus aquae digitum non altior unum,   414
qui lapides inter sistit per strata viarum,
despectum praebet sub terras impete tanto,
a terris quantum caeli patet altus hiatus;
nubila despicere et caelum ut videare videre ⟨et⟩
corpora miranda sub terras abdita caelo.[bb]

[x] "Do you see how the torches toss back their shining hair?"
[y] "and again the nightly torches of the sky which fly on high, do you not see that they trail long tracts of flames behind towards whatever side nature has set them to travel?" Bailey.
[z] "in the night season, then the shining constellations appear"
[aa] "and the torches of heaven that rove through the night and the flying flames" Bailey.
[bb] "and yet a pool of water not deeper than a single fingerbreadth, which lies between the stones of the paved street, af-

We look down and down through the fine spondee of "despectum praebet" to clouds and heavenly bodies hidden in a marvelous way beneath the earth.

We do not know what beach it was that Lucretius immortalized in Book II.374-376.[29] No ancient poet who read these three verses ever forgot them. But the best feature of any echo is that it recalls the original. Nowhere in the whole of the *De Rerum Natura* has the poet demonstrated more strikingly his readiness with the words to express completely his thought and feeling. Here he has given us form and color and sound and motion in a pattern as delicate as lace but as solidly real as the earth itself.

> concharumque genus parili ratione videmus   II.374
> pingere telluris gremium, qua mollibus undis
> litoris incurvi bibulam pavit aequor harenam.[cc]

Cyril Bailey, in his note on II.374, says that here Lucretius turns to "inanimate nature," but in fact Lucretius seems at pains to depict his specimens as anything but "inanimate." At the outset, "concharum genus," "the breed or race of shells," introduces living beings and the word "gremium"[30] suggests that their mother earth is holding them in a warm embrace. Their setting, too, is full of life and motion. At the head of a cove (*litoris incurvi*) in the tideless Mediterranean *pavit* is the perfect term for the light slap of a wavelet on the beach, if we

---

fords us a view beneath the earth to a depth as vast as the high gaping mouth of heaven stretches above the earth; so that you seem to look down on the clouds and the heaven and bodies hidden in the sky beneath the earth—all in magic wise." Bailey.

  [cc] "And in like manner we see the race of shells painting the lap of earth, where with its gentle waves the sea beats on the thirsty sand of the winding shore." Bailey.

accept what we hear and refrain from searching for etymological violence.[31] Nonius, who was no poet, quoted the line with *lavit* and so reduced it to the commonplace version that displaced the manuscript reading in some old editions.[32] *Bibulam harenam* is more than "thirsty sand," though it includes that meaning. There is something in the very shape and sound of the epithet to recall the little bubbles (*bulae*) that when a wave has receded stand for a second or two before they wink out and disappear in the sand.[33] It is the vibration of the shrieking saw with its shuddering blades that comes to us so vividly from Lucretius II.410 f., in the repeated *R* sounds, especially of *horrorem*:

> Ne tu forte putes serrae stridentis acerbum   410
> horrorem constare elementis levibus aeque
> ac musaea mele per chordas organici quae
> mobilibus digitis expergefacta figurant.[dd]

The sound is *acerbum*, and Lucretius explains its contrast with pleasant musical strains by the roughness or smoothness of the atoms that compose them both. As so often with Lucretian passages, a trace appears in Virgil (*Georgics* I.143) but again, as usual, in a totally different connection.[34] Virgil is recording the invention of the saw as a step in human progress:

> tum ferri rigor atque argutae lammina serrae,[ee]

He is not interested in the sound, and so a politer epithet (*argutae*) replaces *stridens* and *horrorem* has disappeared

---

[dd] "lest by chance you may think that the harsh shuddering sound of the squeaking saw is made of particles as smooth as are the melodies of music which players awake, shaping the notes as their fingers move over the strings." Bailey.

[ee] "then the stiffness of iron and the blade of the shrill saw."

with its vibrating *R*'s. *Ferri rigor* is another Lucretian reminiscence from Book 1.492:[35] "cum labefactatus rigor auri solvitur aestu," another instance of widely separated passages from Lucretius brought together in Virgil's mind.

A word at the end of a line exerts a special force, as does *angat* in Lucretius IV.1133. *Angat* is a cruel word, as hard as iron, and emphasized here by following on *floribus*, which is so soft both in sound and meaning:

> medio de fonte leporum   1133
> surgit amari aliquid, quod in ipsis floribus angat.[ff]

The passage in which this line occurs (IV.1121-1140) is one of those (like the seashell verses of II.374-376) that show that if Lucretius had not elected to spend his gifts on the propagation of the faith, Catullus might not hold his undisputed place as master of the Latin lyric. Virgil has of course stored these cadences in his mind.[36]

Lucretius reduplicates the effect of *angat* with the *anxius angor* he uses of a plague victim (VI.1158) and of the mortal sinner who suffers on earth the pangs of the mythical Tityos (III.993):

> quem volucres lacerant atque exest anxius angor.[gg]

Virgil transfers the phrase to Cybele's anxiety for the ships built from her trees (*Aen.* IX.89):

> —nunc sollicitam timor anxius angit[37][hh]

[ff] ". . . from the heart of this fountain of delights wells up some bitter taste to choke them even amid the flowers." Bailey.

[gg] "whom . . . the birds mangle, yea, aching anguish devours him." Bailey.

[hh] ". . . now anxious fear tortures my troubled breast." Fairclough.

Amari is another potent word in IV.1134, which Lucretius apparently values partly for its sound in the verse. In one of his repeated passages (VI.921-935 = IV.217-229), he produces a variant of it in the strange masculine noun *amaror*:

> cum tuimur misceri absinthia, tangit amaror.[ii]
>
> IV.224 or VI.930

It may be one of his happy inventions, since it is certainly more euphonious than *amarities* or *amaritudo*, and it occurs nowhere else except once in Virgil's *Georgics* II.246f., where it is clearly taken over from Lucretius:

> at sapor indicium faciet manifestus et ora[38]
> tristia temptantum sensu torquebit amaror.[jj]

The relation to Lucretius is clarified by a comparison with another passage (II.400f.):

> at contra taetra absinthi natura ferique
> centauri foedo pertorquent ora sapore.[kk]

Virgil, in describing a test for salty soil, is recalling the words of Lucretius about the taste of bitter medicine. Catullus in allusion to a different sort of bitter mixture uses the metrically suitable *amaritiem*:

> multa satis lusi; non est dea nescia nostri   68.17
>   quae dulcem curis miscet amaritiem.[ll]

[ii] "when we behold wormwood . . . mixed, a bitter taste touches it." Bailey.

[jj] "but the taste will tell its tale full plainly, and with its bitter flavor will distort the testers' soured mouths." Fairclough.

[kk] "but on the other hand, the loathsome nature of wormwood and biting centaury set the mouth awry by their noisome taste." Bailey.

[ll] "I have trifled enough; that goddess knows me well, who mingles sweet bitterness with cares."

There is no doubt that Lucretius had a singular understanding of word power and of his own ability to wield
it. It is the basis of the "true poet's violence," which
Jackson Knight recognizes in his use of language.[39] His
conterranei Catullus and Virgil share his gift. It is impossible to believe that Virgil could have responded so
completely to his influence, become so "impregné" as
Ernout puts it,[40] if he had not met the inspiration in the
north, perhaps in the school at Cremona, at the magic
moment of adolescence when poetry first becomes a living force. The history of Roman literature would have
been different if Virgil had first encountered Lucretius
when he had reached Rome as a mature man. He took
Lucretius and Catullus with him to Rome, and those
provincials, neglected in their own day, made their mark
on the Augustans[41] in the next generation.

IV

Lucretius: Northern Landscape and Culture

The scholars who have struggled valiantly to recon-
struct a biography of Lucretius from the inadequate
evidence available divide into two main camps. Of these
one maintains that the poet was a native of Rome and a
member of the patrician tribe of the Lucretii Tricipitini,
whose distinguished career begins in the legendary days
of the kingship.[1] The second differs as widely as possible.[2]
Marx advocated the extreme view that the poet was not
only no Roman but was of servile origin, manumitted
apparently by a Lucretius in Cisalpine Gaul. Without accepting all of his argument, others have at least agreed
that Lucretius was a Transpadane. As was pointed out
above[3] the ancient testimony fails to establish with reasonable certainty anything more than that the life of
Lucretius began in the opening years of the first century
B.C. and ended early in the second half of the same century. Something can be deduced from internal evidence
in the poem itself. As already observed, the style of
Lucretius, and especially the kind and distribution of
his elisions,[4] so compatible with that of the Transpadanes
Catullus and Virgil and so opposed to that of the Roman
Cicero, indicates a northern origin, though how high
or low in the social scale we can only conjecture from
what he tells us of his way of living.

Those who conform to the "orthodox view" in con-
tending that Lucretius is a native and lifelong resident of
the capital ignore the elisions except to brand them as

"awkward and excessive." They maintain that Lucretius displays familiarity with Roman things and institutions.[5] A line often quoted to support this contention is:

conventus hominum pompam convivia pugnas[a]   IV.784

The context concerns the incredible speed with which images of concepts flash into our minds. The list is intentionally a hodge-podge of random concepts entirely unrelated to one another, and no more relevant to Rome than to any other place where people live and carry on their affairs. Yet *conventus hominum* has been taken as a definite allusion to the Roman senate. Again, paved streets[6] are hardly limited to Rome.

It is generally assumed that the theater so beautifully pictured for us (IV.75-83; VI.109) with its flapping awnings shedding their colors on the spectators seated beneath them is a Roman theater. Indeed, it very well may be but there is no certainty. Again the senate is doubtfully represented here since the unfortunate corruption of the text makes it questionable whether any form of the word *patres* belongs in this context (IV.75ff.):

et vulgo faciunt id lutea russaque vela   75
et ferrugina, cum magnis intenta theatris
per malos vulgata trabesque trementia flutant.
namque ibi consessum caveai subter et omnem
scaenai speciem,† patrum matrumque deorum†
inficiunt coguntque suo fluitare colore.   80
et quanto circum mage sunt inclusa theatri
moenia, tam magis haec intus perfusa lepore
omnia corrident correpta luce diei.[b]

---

[a] "gatherings of men, a procession, banquets, battles" Bailey.
[b] "and commonly is this done by awnings yellow and red and purple when stretched over great theatres they flap and flutter,

The awnings were a Campanian invention, but once
introduced were generally adopted.[7] They were first used
in Rome about 70 B.C. in a temporary theater erected for
the Ludi Circenses.[8]

Lucretius mentions the awnings again in VI.109f., where
the sound of the words cleverly suggests the snapping
of the great linen sheets in the wind:

> carbasus ut quondam magnis intenta theatris
> dat crepitum malor inter iactata trabesque.[c]

There are archaeological remains of theaters all across
the Po Valley from Milan to Trieste,[9] and so it seems un-
necessary to place the unlocated theaters of Lucretius
in the capital. He says nothing about the drama but tells
of his pleasure in exhibitions of dancing, which delighted
him so much that they recurred to him in his dreams at
night.[10] He does not speak of gladiatorial shows, though
if he had been living in Rome he could not have escaped
seeing or at least knowing about Caesar's use of them
to please the public in his early political career.[11]

One more claim to Roman associations rests on the
mention of military exercises in *campus* or *campi*, generally taken to mean the Campus Martius. The more de-
tailed of the two passages is II.323-332:

---

spread everywhere on masts and beams. For there they tinge the
assembly in the tiers beneath, and all the bravery of the stage
(and the grey-clad company of the elders) and constrain them
to flutter in their colours. And the more closely are the hoard-
ings of the theatre shut in all around, the more does all the
scene within laugh, bathed in brightness as the light of day is
straitened." Bailey.

[c] "as often an awning stretched over a great theatre gives a
crack, as it tosses among the posts and beams." Bailey.

praeterea magnae legiones cum loca cursu
camporum complent belli simulacra cientes,
fulgor ubi ad caelum se tollit totaque circum   325
aere renidescit tellus subterque virum vi
excitur pedibus sonitus clamoreque montes
icti reiectant voces ad sidera mundi
et circumvolitant equites mediosque repente
tramittunt valido quatientes impete campos,   330
et tamen est quidam locus altis montibus ⟨unde⟩
stare videntur et in campis consistere fulgor.[d]

A closely similar passage in II.40-43a uses much the same
expressions:

Si non forte tuas legiones per loca campi   40
fervere cum videas belli simulacra cientis,
ornatas ⟨que⟩ armis statuas pariterque animatas,
subsidiis magnis et ecum vi constabilitas,
[fervere cum videas classem lateque vagari.][e]   43a

---

[d] "moreover, when mighty legions fill the spaces of the plains
with their chargings, awaking a mimic warfare, and a sheen rises
there to heaven and all the earth around gleams with bronze and
beneath a noise is roused by the mighty mass of men as they
march, and the hills smitten by their shouts hurl back the cries
to the stars of the firmament, and the cavalry wheel round and
suddenly shake the middle of the plains with their forceful onset,
as they scour across them, yet there is a certain spot on the high
hills, whence all seems to be at rest and to lie like a glimmering
mass upon the plains." Bailey.

[e] "unless perchance when you see your legions swarming over
the spaces of the campus (plain) and provoking a mimic war,
when you draw them up equipped with arms, all alike eager for
the fray, strengthened with hosts in reserve and forces of cavalry, when you see the army wandering far and wide in busy
haste." Bailey.

To say nothing of the strange plural in *loca camporum* (324f.), there was not enough open space left in the Campus Martius of Lucretius's day for maneuvers on the scale described here. The *legiones* are overpowering for that place, and the suggestion of cavalry drill is even more out of context (*ecum vi* [43] and *circumvolitant equites* [329]). The word *campus* is a general term for comparatively level lands as opposed to mountainous terrain, and Lucretius uses it often in places where there is obviously no connection with Rome.[12] The *alti montes* from which an unobstructed view of the *campus* is possible are likewise not a feature of the Roman scene, but belong to quite a different setting, which is to be discussed in connection with the dedication (Chapter VI).

Incidental references to warfare do not suggest that Lucretius speaks as a native of the city. Like Catullus he never served in the army. Episodes from the past are drawn from the Persian invasion of Greece or from the second Punic War.[13] Hannibal's coming over the Alps would naturally be a part of oral tradition, familiar to every child in the Po Valley. If Lucretius grew up in Rome his most impressionable years were passed during civil wars, with savage fighting in the streets, with the heads of defeated factions exhibited in the Forum.[14] Even if his family protected him from all this as far as possible, there would be enough in conversations overheard, and especially in the gossip of the servants, to leave indelible impressions on his sensitive mind. There is no trace of these horrors in the poem; those passages cited as such are at most pale literary reflections.

What Lucretius does not say is as important in revealing his background as are his direct statements. For instance, though he speaks frequently of streams and

76

rivers, he never mentions the Tiber,[15] and those he describes without naming are of the rocky-bedded mountain variety. Streams in the neighborhood of Rome are spanned by bridges or ferries, and even the smallest of them are never crossed by fording. If Lucretius tried to cross one of them on horseback in the fashion he describes in IV.420ff., all he would see on looking down (*despeximus*, line 421) would be slow-moving brown water and the horse's legs sinking deeper and deeper into the mud:

denique ubi in medio nobis equus acer obhaesit   420
flumine et in rapidas amnis despeximus undas,
stantis equi corpus transversum ferre videtur
vis et in adversum flumen contrudere raptim,
et quocumque oculos traiecimus omnia ferri
et fluere assimili nobis ratione videntur.[f]   425

Here the horse has "stuck" (*obhaesit*), that is, he has caught his feet in the stones, but we know he will get his balance and go on to the other side. But when his rider looks down during this pause into the rushing water, the horse and all else in view seem to be swept along against the current.

Three of those mountain streams are described for us by the three Transpadane poets who have so much in common:

(1) Catullus 68.57ff.:

[f] "and again, when in midstream our spirited horse has made a dead stop and we look down into the swift water, the force seems to carry the body of the horse (which is standing still) athwart the current and to thrust it upstream at high speed, and wherever we turn our gaze, everything seems to be carried along and swept forward in the same fashion as we ourselves."

Qualis in aerii perlucens vertice montis   57
 rivus muscoso prosilit e lapide
qui, cum de prona praeceps est valle volutus,
 per medium densi transit iter populi,   60
dulce viatori lasso in sudore levamen
 cum gravis exustos aestus hiulcat agros.[g]

Catullus in writing of the mountain stream has made it part of his personal experience and has compared its virtues to the saving help of a friend. Lucretius, on the other hand, has turned from his own time to the picture of primitive man searching for the means of survival in the wilds and has no thought of the river's ending with the "iter densi populi" of Catullus.

(2) Lucretius v.945-953:

at sedare sitim fluvii fontesque vocabant,   945
ut nunc montibus e magnis decursus aquai
claricitat late sitientia saecla ferarum.
denique nota vagis silvestria templa tenebant
nympharum, quibus e scibant umori' fluenta
lubrica proluvie larga lavere umida saxa,   950
umida saxa, super viridi stillantia musco,
et partim plano scatere atque erumpere campo.[h]

[g] "as a rivulet, shining on the summit of an airy mountain, has leapt forth from a mossy stone, when in headlong course along the valley floor, has crossed the path of a thronging people, a welcome relief to the weary traveler when oppressive heat has split the scorched fields."

[h] "but to slake their thirst streams and springs summoned them, even as now the downrush of water from the great mountains loudly summons far and wide the thirsting babes of wild beasts. Or again they dwelt in the woodland haunts of the nymphs, which they had learnt in their wanderings, from which they knew that gliding streams of water washed the wet rocks with bounteous flood, yea washed the wet rocks, as they dripped

(3) Virgil remembered both these passages and echoes of them sound through all his works with characteristically changed application. In *Aeneid* xii.523-525 the river's course is compared to the rush of warriors through the zone of combat:

Aut ubi decursu rapido de montibus altis
dant sonitum spumosi amnes et in aequora current
quisque suum populatus iter.[i]

Years before, in *Eclogue* viii.59f., the same river's rush had been the suicide leap of the shepherd crossed in love:

praeceps aerii specula de montis in undas deferar.[j]

But to return to Lucretius and Rome, the Tiber was not the only omission. He never names a single hill.[16] He never mentions the Forum or the Via Sacra, the Lares and Penates. Vesta and Janus are lacking, although they dominate the heart of the city. It is no Epicurean prejudice that bars them because other gods appear in the course of the poem.[17] Terminus, for example, so important to the country dweller and an archaic survival to the townsman, is mentioned six times.[18] The only myth lovingly developed at some length has a northern setting: it was on the banks of the Po where Phaethon fell and where his sisters shed their amber tears in mourning for him (v.394ff.).[19]

A surprisingly conspicuous place is given to the Great

---

down over the green moss, and here and there welled up and burst forth over the level plain." Bailey.

[i] "or when in swift downrush from high mountains, foaming rivers send out their roar and race into the sea, each having laid waste its own course."

[j] "headlong from a lookout on an airy mountain will I hurl myself into the waves."

Mother of the gods, Magna Mater (II.598-659). The goddess makes a fine appearance with the turreted crown on her head and seated in her chariot under showers of rose petals thrown by the spectators. That the chariot is drawn by lions in her traditional fashion[20] (601: "biiugos agitares leones") is unexpected, and it is difficult to distinguish between the mythology of the ancient poets and a current procession.[21] It is quite clear in any case that there is no hint in this description of any of the distinctively Roman features of her cult as they are given by Ovid in the *Fasti* IV.179-372. There is no reference to the stone brought by ship from Asia Minor and up the Tiber to be housed in a temple on the Palatine, no mention of the *lavatio*, the bathing of the image, no mention of the fact that Roman citizens were forbidden to serve as her priests. It seems probable that what interest Lucretius had in the Magna Mater was due not to Roman associations but to the north where we have evidence of her prominence.[22] Catullus wrote the Attis (63) about one phase of her tradition and his friend Caecilius of Comum composed a poem that Catullus cites in his poem 35.14 and 18. It seems that a Celtic cult of "Matres" prepared the way for her in that region.[23]

A puzzling remark of Lucretius 1.316ff. seems to take us back to the north for explanation:

> tum portas propter aena   316
> signa manus dextras ostendunt attenuari
> saepe salutantum tactu praeterque meantum.[k]

Statues "before the gates" were known in many places.[24] There is an adjective in common use for them in Greek:

[k] "again, beside the city gates bronze statues show that their right hands are being rubbed thin by the touch of those who greet them as they pass by."

"προπυλαῖος." Pausanias IV.334, for instance, mentions one from Messenia, and Varro reports an example from Samothrace (*L.L.* v.58). There is no notice of such a traffic block outside one of the busy gates of Rome, and it seems unlikely that any existed there in Lucretius's day. The Latin epithet *anteportanus* is very rare (only one instance in the Thesaurus). Pascal, page 164, reports it as an epithet of Hercules in an inscription found near Lago Maggiore (*CIL* v.5534). Though the evidence is not very satisfactory, the custom appears rather provincial than Roman.

To leave Rome and retreat to the places where Lucretius was happily at home, we find there is no doubt that he knew and loved the mountain landscape.[25] We have already noted his mountain streams and the rocky-bedded *rivus* he forded on horse-back. He hunted not with beaters and nets in the southern style but by using his keen-scented dog to track the beast to its lair (1.397-416). The *montivagae ferai* were his quarry. The dogs sent ahead (IV.680f.) lead the huntsman wherever the "fissa ferarum ungula" leads them. Lucretius is remembering the wild deer "in the tender grass" which Empedocles describes (frag. 101), but here the soft grass is replaced by hard rock, and we hear in the *G* and *C* sounds the click of their horny little feet against the stones:

> tum fissa ferarum   680
> ungula quo tulerit gressum promissa canum vis
> ducit.[1]

The same dogs that serve their master on the hills are also his companions at home, and he observes both them

---

[1] "then the strength of dogs sent on before leads on the hunters whithersoever the cloven hoof of the wild beasts has turned its steps." Bailey.

and his horses with understanding sympathy. There is a fine passage in v.1062-72 where, after a few words about the sounds uttered by wild beasts, he describes in vivid detail how his great Molossian hounds express their feelings in a language of their own, with special voice and gesture for threatening, in cringing from a blow, barking on guard duty, and most touching of all when they play with their puppies, feigning to bite them, but never closing their jaws, growling affectionately when they toss them with their paws.

From the dogs he passes on to the horses with the varied neighing of the breeding stallion, so different from its ordinary sound.

None of this reflects the life style of the city dweller. One imagines Lucretius in a simple but comfortable villa with easy access not only to his beloved mountains but to the seashore, which he seems to know as intimately. We have already mentioned the charming picture of the colored shells and the bubbles on the sand at the head of some unidentified cove (II.374ff.). He also speaks of the salt taste we find in our mouths when we are busy in some way on the shore (IV.222f.) and of the moisture absorbed by garments hung up near the beach (I.305):

denique fluctifrago suspensae in litore vestes
uvescunt.[m]

The break at the water-line of the oars alongside an anchored vessel is another point he has noticed (IV. 438ff.). The congested and noisy port of Ostia seems an unlikely background for these quiet and entirely incidental observations. He must have known some tranquil little harbor in his own neighborhood where he occasion-

[m] "once more, garments hung up upon the shore, where the waves break, grow damp." Bailey.

ally also came and went on board the small sailing ships of his day.[26]

There are many indications that Lucretius thought naturally of life as carried on in the lands pressing, so to speak, against the high mountains. He imagines primitive man schooling the trees to recede higher up the slopes to leave the lower ground free for vineyards and other cultivation (v.1370ff.):

> inque dies magis in montem succedere silvas
> cogebant infraque locum concedere cultis.[n]

He obviously enjoyed climbing in the mountains with his friends and his dogs, sometimes for hunting but partly at least for the satisfaction of successful physical effort and the interest of exploring nooks and crannies on the heights. In iv.577-79 we share the experience of comrades who have lost sight of one another and hear the echo of their own voices as they shout at the top of their lungs to maintain contact:

> sex etiam aut septem loca vidi reddere voces,
> unam cum iaceres: ita colles collibus ipsi
> verba repulsantes iterabant dicta referre.[o]

He succumbs here to the temptation to record the belief of the country people thereabouts to say that "capripedes satyros nymphasque" possess these places, along with fauns and Pan himself, who *unco labro* (with hooked or outcurving lip) runs over the holes of his reeds while

---

[n] "and day by day they would constrain the woods more and more to retire up the mountains, and to give up the land beneath to tilth." Bailey.

[o] "I have seen places give back even six or seven cries, when you sent forth but one: so surely did one hill beat back the words to another and re-echo what was said again and again." Bailey.

he nods his wreath of wild pine in time to the music. Of course he catches himself as he does after speaking of Phaethon and the Great Mother to explain that all this is pure imagination, but it is clear that like all children and poets he enjoys "cetera de genere hoc monstra ac portenta" (IV.590) during his momentary lapses from "vera ratio."

Without central heating, as many of us know from experience, the words for a Roman winter are "Ah bitter chill it was," but there is never the hard freezing that Lucretius seems to have endured in his mountain winters. He has a particular talent for describing cold, unmatched as far as I know anywhere else in Latin literature. In listing what can gather in the clouds above us, he writes:

> omnia, prorsum   VI.528
> omnia, nix venti grando gelidaeque pruinae
> et vis magna geli, magnum duramen aquarum,[27]
> et mora qua fluvios passim refrenat aventis.[p]

The river, in the language applicable to *equus acer* is reined in from its eager dash, a striking enough metaphor, but the outstanding Lucretian touch in the passage is *duramen* in the second line, where it is called "the great hardener of waters."[28]

One more out of many telling examples where every word has special force is I.355:

> —rigidum permanat frigus ad ossa.[q]

Snow appears often in the verses, sometimes with un-

[p] "all, yes all of them, snow, winds, hail, chill hoar-frosts, and the great force of ice, that great hardener of waters, the curb which everywhere reins in the eager streams."

[q] "stiffening cold seeps through to the bones."

expected connection as in the Great Mother's procession, where the crowds along her way give her gold and silver (II.627): "ninguntque rosarum floribus."[r] Lucretius had often walked through falling snow and had missed none of its beauty. He had clearly seen the flake with its intricate structure against the background of his dark cloak and had watched the snowflake's fall so that he knew it did not drop straight down, but descended in steps, drop and glide, drop and glide until it reached the ground. He distilled his experiences in one captivating episode in III.20 and 21. The lines are part of a description of the gods' dwelling place, a picture based on the *Odyssey*. The critics in general ignore these verses except to remark that they "imitate" Homer.[29] In describing the mythically perfect climate "where falls not rain nor hail nor any snow," the Greek says nothing more about snow than the matter of fact "οὐκ ἐπιπίλναται" ["does not come near"], but Lucretius gives us first (line 20) the formation of the flake by the frost crystals growing together, and then the white fall with the word breaks marking its stages, glide, drop, glide, drop, in *cana cadens* until it comes to rest with the softest possible word of marring, *violat*:

> —neque nix acri concreta pruina
> cana cadens violat.[30] [s]

Scattered throughout the six books are various references to children, from the new-born baby through all the stages of young childhood and adolescence.[31] Lucretius has watched them with the same interest and sympathy he shows toward animals. It is Catullus again

[r] "snow the goddess with rose blossoms."

[s] "nor does the snowflake, congealed with sharp freezing, with its white fall mar their peace."

who is closest to him in bringing a young child to life in
the little Torquatus on his mother's lap stretching out his
hands to his father and smiling with half-parted lips
(61.216ff.):

> Torquatus volo parvulus
> matris e gremio suae
> porrigens teneras manus
> dulce rideat ad patrem
> semihiante labello.[t]

There is nothing to compare with this in all Roman
literature since Dido's little Aeneas (*Aeneid* IV.328f.)
means less for his own sake than for his parents:

> siquis mihi parvulus aula
> luderet Aeneas qui te tamen ore referret.[u]

It may be that in the simpler provincial households adults
and children were less completely separated by staffs of
paedagogi and other servants.

After all, Lucretius has left us a fairly complete picture
of his environment and his way of life. He knew a town
(though what town we do not know), had heard the local
orator harangue the assembled people, had seen religious
processions, had watched artisans at work, had even seen
at close range the driving of piles in water,[32] an ancient
and much used skill in the north country. But he belonged
most of all in a villa whose lands crowded against the
nearby mountain wall and stole some of its lower slope
by pushing back the forest. He hunted for game and

---

[t] "I wish a little Torquatus from his mother's arms to stretch
out soft hands to his father, while he smiles sweetly with half-
parted lips."

[u] "if in my hall a tiny Aeneas were playing who would yet
recall you in his features."

climbed for pleasure among the rocky heights. He had easy access to the sea, which he knew well in all its moods. Rome was hardly a part of it all. The soft contours of the Alban Hills, the deep-cut muddy rivers of the Campagna were not his familiar landscape. The places and institutions any Rome-dweller (like Horace, for instance) could not avoid mentioning, never came to his mind. He knew from books (probably from his school days) the legends and tales of the old city. He knew the Rome of his own day perhaps from a somewhat similar type of hearsay. He lived withdrawn from the life of the capital with his books and his horses and dogs, writing in a style a little out of fashion and scarcely knowing how to get a hearing for the message he felt he must convey to the Latin-reading world.

V

Nepos and Cicero

There could hardly be a worse time for bringing out a difficult and lengthy poem than the years when Lucretius was finishing his *De Rerum Natura*. His friend and *conterraneus*, Cornelius Nepos was the natural person to whom he might appeal for help.[1] Fronto (Loeb ii.168) says Nepos was a publisher, and, in spite of his provincial origin and associations, he seems to have been well-known in Rome and was a friend of Cicero and Atticus. Unfortunately he did not succeed in generating the desired publicity, as we know very well from the fact that the name of Lucretius is mentioned only twice in his own generation. Of those two notices, one certainly, and the other probably, came after the poet's death. The first is included in the Nepos life of Atticus (12.4):

> Idem L. Julium Calidum, quem post Lucreti Catullique mortem, multo elegantissimum poetam nostram tulisse aetatem vere videor posse contendere, neque minus virum bonum optimisque artibus eruditum, post proscriptionem equitum propter magnas eius Africanas possessiones in proscriptorum numerum a P. Volumnio, praefecto fabrum Antonii absentem relatum expedivit.[2a]

[a] "The same (Atticus) rescued Lucius Julius Calidus who, after the death of Lucretius and Catullus, I think I can maintain was the most polished poet our age produced, and no less a fine man and one trained in the best arts, after the proscription of the knights, on account of his extensive properties in Africa, included in his absence in the number of the proscribed by P. Volumnius, Antony's prefect."

88

The second notice is a comment in a letter from Cicero to his brother Quintus, which because of its rarity and the prestige of Cicero's name has been the subject of almost endless discussion (*Ad Q. Fr.* ii.10.4):[3] "Lucreti poemata, ut scribis, ita sunt—multis luminibus ingenii, multae tamen artis. Sed cum veneris—Virum te putabo si Sallusti *Empedoclea* legeris, hominem non putabo."[b]

It may be not only that Nepos was responsible for the passage quoted above from his *Life of Atticus* but that he was in a way the cause of Cicero's mention of Lucretius in the letter to his brother.

The original dedication around which Lucretius had built the whole fabric of his *De Rerum Natura* had to be abandoned for practical reasons.[4] The change (in 55 B.C.) was a difficult one and in itself doubtless a crushing disappointment to the writer. Not the least trying of the bad elements in the situation was the problem of finding a substitute when nobody was entirely adequate and few men then alive could be thought of as even possible. Cicero was at this time restored to Rome and outwardly at least in a fairly secure position, with his exile well in the past. In his existing correspondence there are some traces of communication with Nepos, and we have it on the authority of Macrobius (ii.1.14) that the collections once contained two books of letters to Nepos. If this series had not been lost, we might have something better than our present conjectures to solve the enigma of Lucretius. Even without such certain evidence we can learn from a thorough study of its context and setting that the famous "judgment" of Cicero on Lucretius in the letter

[b] "The poems of Lucretius are, as you write, marked by many flashes of genius, yet show much technical skill. But more of that when you come—I'll think you no mere human, but a hero if you read the *Empedoclea* of Sallust."

to Quintus is of much less consequence than has been assumed. What help Nepos may have asked of Cicero in the difficult problem of bringing out the *De Rerum Natura* we can not say. With Cicero's well-known opposition to Epicurean doctrine it is hardly possible that he proposed Cicero's assuming the role of an active sponsor of the work. It may have been nothing more than a request to channel the manuscript into the workshop of Atticus to be copied for circulation. Whatever it was, it had no effect because we can find no sign that Lucretius received any notice whatever at this time in Rome.

The neglect of both Lucretius and Catullus by their contemporaries is conspicuous enough to give rise to the frequently repeated suggestion of a "conspiracy of silence" ("congiura del silenzio") against them.[5] There is no proof of any deliberate suppression. The idea of a ban imposed on them seems a desperate attempt to explain by pure conjecture the surprising fact that "both Lucretius and Catullus were neglected and missed the honor due them."[6] There may be nothing more sinister here than the usual Roman tendency to disregard the outlander and a resultant lack of awareness of what was taking place outside their narrow circle. Bignone (II.165) is probably correct in his opinion that Cicero and his brother had no realization of the greatness of Lucretius.

In the records preserved to us, Cicero is the first to mention the name of Lucretius, in the letter to his brother Quintus. The basic difficulty in understanding the fairly simple passage is that we tend to seize too eagerly on the few words relating to *Lucreti poemata* without considering the full Ciceronian context.

The letter in question[7] is one of a series written in the late winter of 54 B.C. Though the correspondence is for us one-sided, the general nature of what Quintus contributed to it is quite clear. Cicero and his family have lived through the bitterness of his exile, the triumph of his return, and the wretched realization that those whom he considered his own party (the *optimates* or the *boni*, as he calls them) are not only powerless to direct the course of events but more than willing to sacrifice him to what seem their own immediate interests. He has come, through humiliation and disillusionment we can never measure, to renounce some of his well-known convictions and support the Triumvirate. He is aware of the damage to his brother's fortunes from the simple fact of their kinship, and he has not forgotten the support of Quintus during his exile.[8] Like the Romans in general, he is shockingly ready to look upon the provinces as a means of repairing losses, and he is trying to use his temporarily cordial relations with Caesar to ensure prosperity and distinction for Quintus. Quintus has the prospect of going to Gaul as Caesar's *legatus*, but he is feeling anxious and insecure until the arrangements can be completed. Sihler (*T.A.P.A.* 28 [1897] 43-44) assumes Quintus is seeing to some building project. He had left not long before this letter, and Cicero expects him to return soon. He is detained for the moment in some suburban residence out of touch with the daily gossip of the city and dependent for news and constant reassurance upon Marcus, who does his best to keep up the spirits of his younger brother. Unfortunately there is nothing positive and encouraging to report. The correspondence with Caesar about the appointment has been delayed by accidental damage to a letter in transit, the senate is accomplishing little or nothing, and there are constant reminders that personal enemies are still active and alert. Short-tempered and impatient by nature, Quintus is not tolerating his suspense very successfully.[9] He sends a sort of "special delivery" letter to Marcus written on *codicilli,* waxed leaves to be erased and reinscribed with the answer while messengers wait. Flurried by the peremptory and ill-tempered demand for an immediate reply, Marcus forgets to report the mishap to his letter to Caesar and is at a loss for matter. He proceeds with the lightest touch he can manage, to "ramble on" (alucinari) with such bits of talk as the brothers might exchange if they were together. He begins with a jesting (and somewhat unfeeling) allusion to the people of Tenedos, who have failed in their petition for greater independence; second, a district of Lydia has spoken gratefully of Quintus. Here the themes seem to be running out, and Marcus inserts a general promise to write a daily report, however trivial ("etiam si nihil erit, tamen scribam cotidie aliquid"), and pledges himself to be on hand for a matter of business affecting both Quintus and Atticus. Here would be a natural end for the letter, but the *codicilli* still show too much empty space and the messenger waits.[10] As an afterthought Marcus adds the above mentioned inconsequential literary items: "Lucreti poemata, ut scribis, ita sunt—multis luminibus ingenii, multae tamen artis. Sed cum veneris—Virum te putabo si Sallusti *Empedoclea* legeris, hominem non putabo."

Another letter of the same series (II.13.3f.) offers a parallel for such off-hand literary comments in the absence of serious news: "Omnia colligo ut novi scribam aliquid ad te. Sed ut vides res me ipsa deficit. Itaque ad Callisthenem et ad Philistum redeo."[e] Here too he condemns one writer and praises the other.

To close a letter with bits of criticism is an old trick of

[e] "I am collecting every scrap so as to send you some fresh news, but as you see, matter is lacking. So I return to Callisthenes and Philistus."

Cicero's as we see from letters to Atticus written as long before as 59 B.C. (*Ad Att.* II.22.7): "Libros Alexandri neglegentis hominis et non boni poetae, sed tamen non inutilis, tibi remisi."[11d]

Obviously this literary chitchat is used as a space filler and a distraction from the anxieties of the moment. Thus the comments on Lucretius and Sallust are of no importance in themselves, but with these additions the *codicilli* now look adequately covered. They are sealed and the messenger departs, leaving Marcus relieved for the time being of his brother's importunities.

A day or two after receiving a reply that evidently showed Quintus restored to good humor, Marcus writes (*Ad Q. Fr.* II.11, edition Tyrell and Purser, 133): "Gaudeo tibi iucundas esse meas litteras,"[e] a remark that suggests a jesting overtone in the message sent back on the *codicilli*. Nothing is so elusive as a joke or a *double entendre*, and it is hard for us to understand what Quintus could have found in the letter not only to change his mood immediately but to keep him light-hearted for days to come. Cicero continues this second letter with some scenes in the senate and explains why Quintus has not heard from Caesar (*Ad Q. Fr.* II.11.4): "De Caesare fugerat me ad te scribere. Video enim quas tu litteras exspectaris. Sed ille scripsit ad Balbum, fasciculum illum epistularum, in quo fuerat et mea et Balbi, totum sibi aqua madidum redditum esse, ut ne illud quidem sciat meam fuisse aliquam epistulam."[f] So Marcus has sent on

---

[d] "I have returned to you the books of Alexander, a careless fellow and no good as a poet, but perhaps with his uses."

[e] "I am glad that you found my letter entertaining."

[f] "I forgot to write you about Caesar; for I see what kind of letter you were looking for. But he (Caesar) wrote to Balbus that the bundle of letters, which included those from me and

to Caesar a copy of the same letter and he assures Quintus "Litterae quidem ad id quod exspectas, fere cum tuo reditu iungentur."[g] This is allowing time for Caesar to receive the replacement for the lost letter and to get his answer to Rome before the expected arrival of Quintus in the city.

Obviously the *poemata* of Lucretius have already dropped from their minds along with Sallust's boring screed on Empedocles and the other trivia of the first letter. They are concentrating on practical affairs. But what was so *iucundum* about the Lucretius letter? Cicero's reply to the third letter shows Quintus still in a relaxed frame of mind.[12]

In their eagerness to make the most of any light on the obscurity of Lucretius, scholars have studied and restudied the one sentence referring to him. Why *poemata*? The word seems inappropriate to a long, sustained work like the *De Rerum Natura*, though we can not be sure that it could not be so applied. It seems more likely to be used of short poems or extracts from a longer composition.[13] However that may be, the whole context of letters II.10 to 13 suggests that Cicero introduces the famous "judgment" on Lucretius not for its importance, but for its unimportance, for a remoteness from the current problems comparable to the remoteness of Tenedos and the Magnetes of Sipylus in Lydia. Though the casual nature of the reference was recognized many years ago,[14] discussion goes on and is at times very interesting. Scholars have continued to torment not only the term *poemata*

---

from Balbus, was delivered to him so water-soaked that he did not know there was a letter from me."

[g] "The letter dealing with what you are waiting to hear will get here about the same time you do."

94

but still more the rather pointless bit that follows it:
"multis luminibus ingenii, multae tamen artis." This con-
veys so little as it stands that some editors have been
driven to rewrite it according to their conjectures, in-
serting *non* before *multis* or *multae*, or else getting rid of
the troublesome *tamen*. There is no need to tamper with
the text since the manuscript record is clear. As it stands,
it suggests a parody of a literary criticism in a stock form
with a balance or opposition of *ingenium* and *ars* pivoted
on *tamen*. The cliché is a convenient substitute for
thoughtful analysis and can be applied almost anywhere
with a satisfyingly pompous effect like "a tale of little
meaning, though the words are strong." This interpretation suits the tone of the letter as a whole and of the
series of which it forms a part. It is not made less probable
by the common use of the terms *ingenium* and *ars* as
Grundelemente to place whatever writer you choose in
his proper pigeon hole.[15] Horace (*Ars Poetica* 295ff.)
cites Democritus:

> Ingenium misera quia fortunatius arte
> credit et excludit sanos Helicone poetas
> Democritus.[h]

Also in *Ars Poetica* 408ff., Horace uses the opposition
again, but shows his typical tendency to echo the idea
rather than the word:

> Natura fierit laudabile carmen an arte
> quaesitum est: ego nec studium sine divite vena
> nec rude quid prosit video ingenium: alterius sic
> altera poscit opem res et coniurat amice.[i]

[h] "Because Democritus believes that native talent is a greater
boon than wretched art, and shuts out from Helicon poets in
their sober senses. . . ." Fairclough.

[i] "Often it is asked whether a praiseworthy poem be due to

The old cliché *ingenium* vs. *ars* comes out less baldly here where Horace states his view that both are necessary, that natural gift and technical discipline must work as partners to produce a worthy poem.

Ovid judges that Ennius makes up by *ingenium* for want of *ars* (*Trist.* II.424: "Ennius ingenio maximus, arte rudis"); but that the opposite is true of Callimachus, "quamvis ingenio non valet, arte valet" (*Amores* 1.15.13). He grants Lucretius greatness in both (*Am.* 1.15.23-24; *Tristia* II.425) and prophesies that he will live until the earth itself perishes.

Ars and *ingenium* as stock terms in criticism did not cease with Ovid and were doubtless already well worn when Cicero used them. There may be an added point in attributing the pretentious commonplace to Quintus ("ut scribis"), who could perhaps recognize a parody of the solemn manner of somebody familiar to both the brothers, Cornelius Nepos perhaps, who was obviously an admirer of Lucretius and may have been boring on the subject. We know that Cicero fancied himself as a wit and was never happier than when making a laughing stock of somebody (see *Ad Q. Fr.* II.12 for a scene in the senate). Such an interpretation suits the tone of the letter as a whole and of the series in which it occurs.

The clumsy Latinity of the "judgment," especially the lack of balance before and after *tamen*, which has challenged the ingenuity of emending editors is certainly not characteristic of Cicero's style and may be either a quo-

---

nature or to art. For my part, I do not see of what avail is either study, when not enriched by nature's vein, or native wit, if untrained, so truly does each claim the other's aid, and make with it a friendly league." Fairclough.

tation from Nepos or a parody of his manner. Either would be instantly recognized and greeted with amusement by Quintus, who had probably suffered equally with his brother from the persistent attempts of Nepos to force Lucretius on their attention. The remark about Julius Calidus, quoted above on page 88, is enough to show how Nepos sometimes expressed himself.

Cicero had probably read at least parts (poemata) of the *De Rerum Natura*, including, one might suppose, the beautiful *Proemium* and other purple patches. Since such passages contain comparatively little Epicurean doctrine and are free of the stylistic traits that would displease Cicero in the work as a whole, he recognized them as showing genuine inspiration, but the stress of his own affairs prevented any permanent impression.

This letter to Quintus is the only support to be found for St. Jerome's assertion that Cicero "emendavit" the books Lucretius had composed in the lucid intervals of his madness; but the tradition that Cicero did indeed "edit" the work is persistent. St. Jerome uses the word *emendare* also for the part Varius and Tucca played in bringing out Virgil's text, which they left very much as they found it with its unfinished lines but with possibly some omissions. The term occurs again in a letter to Atticus (ii.16.4), where Cicero says that Quintus has asked him "ut annales suos emendem et edam." Here as combined with *edam* it apparently means to read through and arrange to "bring out," i.e. arrange for copying for publication. It is possible that the Lucretius text, or parts of it, passed through Cicero's hands on its way to the workshop of Atticus, but hardly that he undertook the task of what we now call "editing." He was much occupied at the time with matters detached from philosophy, when in the country, by writing his *De Republica* "spissum sane opus et operosum"[j] (*Ad Q. Fr.* II.14.1), and when in the city with senate meetings and business in the law courts ("Sic enim habeto numquam me a causis et iudiciis districtiorem fuisse,"[k]*Ad Q. Fr.* II.16.1). Worst of all there hung over him day and night the insecurity of the times and the besetting anxieties about what the next turn might be in public affairs. Such pressures would leave little time and energy for a serious project of "editing" a long and difficult work left unfinished by its author and dealing in a passionate missionary spirit with a system to which Cicero was openly and consistently hostile, in spite of warm friendly relations with some followers of the school.[16] The hard fact is that Cicero never mentioned Lucretius again, though the occasion to do so arose more than once. In the *Tusculan-Disputations* (1.5) he states flatly that Latin writings have contributed nothing to philosophy, "Philosophia iacuit usque ad hanc aetatem nec ullum habuit lumen litterarum Latinarum, quae illustranda et excitanda nobis est."[l] Ironically "lumen litterarum Latinarum" seems an excellent characterization of the *De Rerum Natura*, which he here ignores.

Since Cicero was really interested only in the ethical aspect of any philosophical system, it is possible that he had not only never read the whole work but that he may not have been fully aware of its scope and intention. Some have suggested that he considered it only as poetry and not as science or philosophy at all. The Epicureans es-

[j] "a complex task, to be sure, and one requiring much work."

[k] "So then be sure that I have never been more tied up with cases and trials."

[l] "Philosophy has lain neglected up to this time and has had no illumination from Latin literature: it must be raised up into the light by me."

pecially disapproved of poetry, and Cicero puts into the mouth of Torquatus, the Epicurean spokesman in the *De Finibus*, a clear statement of their attitude toward the poets (1.72): "in quibus nulla solida utilitas omnisque puerilis est delectatio."[m] Catullus, who composed his famous wedding song (61) for the same Torquatus, might have thought he had poor thanks for his offering. But Torquatus was dead, and Cicero could make him say what he chose. By setting Torquatus up only to be knocked down in the argument of the *De Finibus*, he may have been savoring a long-deferred revenge for the *Pro Sulla* trial, for Cicero was not one to suffer ridicule gladly though he enjoyed mocking others.[17]

How soon he had completely forgotten the flash of genius in some pieces of provincial verse he shows by a letter to Memmius in 51 B.C. (*Ad Fam.* XIII.1), several years after Lucretius died and he himself supposedly brought out the poem. Memmius, then in exile, had while in Athens acquired the house and garden of Epicurus. Cicero writes at the request of Atticus to ask him to turn it over to Patro and his misguided Epicureans who look upon it as a sacred place. Cicero is evidently beguiling Memmius with every device he can conjure up, and yet it does not occur to him to mention the dedication to him of the Lucretian *De Rerum Natura*.

It is not only by Cicero that Lucretius is neglected. Cassius, a convert to Epicureanism, in writing to Cicero in 45 B.C., names only Catius and Amafinius as representatives of the school in Latin, though he is defending the system against Cicero's ridicule and threatens to retaliate by sending some "rusticos Stoicos" who would by con-

[m] "that they have no practical worth and it is altogether childish to take pleasure in them."

99

trast make Catius and Amafinius appear like Athenians. Lucretius would have given him better support.

Whatever the Romans may have failed to recognize in Lucretius, his *conterranei* knew and appreciated his genius. Doubtless Cornelius Nepos did what he could, but was not powerful enough to arrest the attention of men too distracted by the threats of the current political upheavals and their own personal danger to realize the full significance of a new work from an unknown poet. Perhaps the persistence of Nepos even antagonized them. Fortunately there was another *conterraneus*, still a boy when Lucretius died, but destined to provide the bridge over which both Catullus and Lucretius could pass from their Republican obscurity to recognition from the Augustans and the later Roman poets. This was the Mantuan, Publius Vergilius Maro.

VI

The Change of Dedication

As an obscure provincial, living some distance away
from the intellectual exchanges of the capital, Lucretius required a sponsor to introduce his work, a "big
name" to catch the attention of the public. There is no
indication that he needed any material aid such as Maecenas gave to Horace, for instance, but the necessity was
at least as pressing, since Lucretius felt he had a mission
to fulfill in bringing the saving message of Epicurus to the
Romans in their own language.[1] It was not difficult to
decide where to turn, but the first thought was not of
Gaius Memmius, to whom the work as we now have it
is dedicated. There is nothing new in the idea that Memmius was an "afterthought."[2]

It was Julius Caesar, who had been a hero to the
Transpadanes from his early career when, on his return
from his quaestorship in Spain, he had passed through
their district and had made his first attempt to extend to
them the same rights of citizenship as were already enjoyed by the people south of the Po.[3] Though the efforts
were for the time being unsuccessful, they had the effect
of making him well-known and well-liked throughout
the region. The quaestor's visit was in fact the beginning
of a life-long relation of friendly patronage on Caesar's
part and an almost hero-worshipping attitude on the part
of the Transpadanes.[4]

It was in the same year of his quaestorship (68 B.C.)
that Caesar at home in the capital delivered the famous

funeral oration for his father's sister Julia, the widow of Marius. Suetonius[5] has preserved the essential part of the speech, which was so widely known that doubtless Lucretius had read it or at least heard of its content:

> Amitae meae Juliae maternum genus ab regibus ortum, paternum cum dis immortalibus coniunctum est. Nam ab Anco Marcio sunt Marcii Reges, quo nomine fuit mater; a Venere Julii, cuius gentis familia est nostra. Est ergo in genere et sanctitas regum, qui plurimum inter homines pollent, et caerimonia deorum quorum ipsi in potestate sunt reges.[a]

There are some indications that Lucretius was familiar with the text of Caesar's speech, besides the all-important "Aeneadum genetrix" with which he opens the *De Rerum Natura* and declares the descent of the Julian *gens* from Venus. Ancus Marcius is the only Roman king Lucretius mentions (III.1025), and the name may well have been impressed on his mind by its prominence in the oration; there seems no other reason for singling out this one of the seven kings, since he seems chiefly distinguished for losing the power to the Etruscans. The lines following the mention of Ancus in Book III bear some vague resemblance to the words of Caesar, but remarks about the power of kings are too commonplace to permit us to infer any special connection. However,

---

[a] "On her mother's side my Aunt Julia's family was descended from kings, and on her father's it was connected with the immortal gods. For the name Marcius Rex, which was her mother's, was from Ancus Marcius and the Julian line, from which our family came, from Venus. There is, then, in her family tree, both the royal prerogative of kings who have the supreme power over human beings, and also the rites of the gods to whose authority the kings themselves are subject."

there is nothing vague about the connection of *Aenea-dum*, a form by the way, which seems to be used here for the first time in Latin. The members of the *gens Julia* are the Aeneades par excellence, as the direct descendants of Aeneas, son of Anchises and Venus. Not only does the family assert this claim, but there are repeated references to it from others, sometimes tongue in cheek, as when Caelius in a letter to Cicero[6] alludes to Caesar as "Venere prognatus." Velleius, II.41.1, attests the descent from Venus quite seriously. Ovid, *Fasti* IV.36-40, 57-60, shows that the Augustans carried on the tradition. Indeed Augustus himself attached some importance to it.

Julius Caesar was by no means the first of his family to claim divine origin. About 88 or 90 B.C. another member of the *gens*, Lucius Caesar, who held the office of censor, conferred some tokens of recognition on Ilium, the town where his exalted forebears founded the Julian line.[7] At the time when Lucius Caesar made his pious gesture, Lucretius was a young child in a small provincial place and surely knew nothing of an occurrence that made little stir in the world, but the well-publicized oration of 68 B.C. was another matter. However, Lucretius had already died when Julius Caesar himself visited Ilium after the battle of Pharsalus in 48 and made the town politically autonomous and exempt from taxation.

After his consulship in 59 Caesar took over Gaul as his province and went north with an army to begin the conquest of Gaul beyond the Alps. After his campaign he regularly withdrew to winter quarters in the Cisalpine valley,[8] where he enlisted new foot soldiers for his legions and also squadrons of cavalry from the skillful horsemen of Germany, Spain, and Gaul. The people became accustomed to the sight and sound of his troops being drilled and of his veterans marching through the valley from Aquileia to the western passes by which they would go out to the new season of warfare. Those descriptions of *legiones* and *equites* in Lucretius that have been mistakenly set in the Campus Martius in Rome[9] were undoubtedly drawn from the wide *campi* available for such exercises where the poet had seen them in his own valley.

si non forte tuas legiones per loca campi   II.40-46
fervere cum videas belli simulacra cientis,
ornatas ⟨que⟩ armis statuas pariterque animatas,   [43]
subsidiis magnis et ecum vi constabilitas,   [42]
[fervere cum videas classem lateque vagari,][10]   [43a]

praeterea magnae legiones cum loca cursu   II.323
camporum complent belli simulacra cientes,
fulgor ubi ad caelum se tollit totaque circum   325
aere renidescit tellus subterque virum vi
excitur pedibus sonitus clamoreque montes
icti reiectant voces ad sidera mundi
et circumvolitant equites mediosque repente
tramittunt valido quatientes impete campos;   330
et tamen est quidam locus altis montibus ⟨unde⟩
stare videntur et in campis consistere fulgor.[11]

Lucretius has carefully chosen the words to evoke the ground-shaking, rhythmic tramp of men and horses, the noise of their shouts, and the bright gleams reflected from their arms. The voices echoed back from mountainsides do not suggest the confined limits of the Campus Martius, and still less does that high point from which a spectator might see in the distance all that seething mass of men and horses as a motionless spot of brightness.

Near the beginning of the poem (1.84-101) there is a digression to introduce the sacrifice of Iphianassa (Iphigenia) as an illustration of what evil may be wrought in the name of religion.[12] Out of all the possible instances Lucretius probably chose this because, as a daughter's tragedy, it might appeal to Caesar whose only legitimate child was a dearly loved daughter, Julia. There is nothing to make it specially significant for Memmius, and it now stands as a digression without much connection with its context.

In characterizing different climates of north, south, east, and west, his northern point is Britain (VI.1106f.). This again recalls the name of Caesar and his recent invasion of that island in 55 B.C.

According to Hirtius (*B.G.* V.51 and *B.C.* III.81) this achievement was acclaimed in Gallia and Caesar apparently valued the feeling the inhabitants showed for him. Probably this is the reason why he took so seriously the lampoons that Catullus wrote against him and that he claimed were libelous. Caesar was too shrewd to believe that what Catullus wrote would have much influence in Rome, but since the poet was well-connected in his home territory the circulation of his verses in Gallia might seriously impair the image Caesar had acquired there. Certainly he went out of his way to establish a more friendly relation with the young poet from Verona, and Catullus seems to have been won over without much difficulty.[13] As proof of his change of heart we have his poem 11 (lines 9-12) with its reference to Caesar's conquest of Britain and the land beyond the Alps.

R. F. Dale[14] has collected some striking echoes of Lucretian lines in Caesar's own writing. They seem to show that Caesar had read the *De Rerum Natura* and found some passages sufficiently impressive to make him remember and repeat the phrases. The first is, as we might cynically have expected, from the Proemium, 1.43: "tali-

bus in rebus communi desse saluti." This appears in *B.G.*
v.33 as: "nulla in re communi saluti deerat." However,
Caesar did not stop with the beginning. Other instances
occur from Lucretius II.358, IV.1017, V.226, 740, 1066.
Nobody will ever know how far the opening words
"Aeneadum genetrix" influenced him to exchange Venus
Victrix, who had given him his winning war-cry at
Pharsalus in 48, for Venus Genetrix when he dedicated
the temple in the Forum Julium.[15]

Why, if Lucretius had dedicated his work to Caesar
as the most desirable sponsor, did he shift to Memmius at
the price of a considerable amount of recasting? It is not
difficult, strange to say, to find a reason that would in-
duce the poet to make the changes, painful and dis-
heartening as the decision must have been to him. In 56
B.C. the Triumvirate of Caesar, Pompey, and Crassus met
at Luca while Caesar was on the Italian side of the Alps
for his usual winter visit. There it was agreed that Pompey and Crassus were to be consuls for the second time in
the following year and Caesar's term in Gaul was to be
extended for another five years. The law by which the
extension was effected was actually passed and made public in 55 and it was then that the devastating news could
reach Lucretius. Caesar was to be in the wilds of north-
western Europe for five years and so unable to give
Lucretius any help in launching his work in the great
world of Rome. Certainly Lucretius needed no love potion to drive him to self-destruction,[16] but it seems clear
that he courageously made the best of a bad situation and
accepted a second best choice. He was probably encour-
aged by his *conterraneus* Cornelius Nepos, who may even
have suggested the substitute. Memmius, though not an
Aenead strictly speaking, claimed descent from Mnes-

theus, a companion of Aeneas. He belonged to an old plebeian family and was accepted in Roman society. He had
shown a generous interest in poets[17] and at the time was
working for the consulship, so that he would not be likely to absent himself from the capital. He had taken two
young Transpadanes, Catullus and Cinna, to Bithynia
when he went out as governor of the province after his
praetorship.

On the surface he seemed an answer to prayer, but
Nepos may have had an uneasy conscience in view of
the personal reputation of Memmius. Lucretius, leading
the retired life of a provincial gentleman and scholar with
an Epicurean aversion to politics, was an innocent in his
judgment on the leaders of public affairs in Rome[18] and
would not realize how few could be found to say a good
word for his proposed sponsor.[19] With his misgivings
Nepos may have turned to Catullus as a friend who
would understand the entire situation, acquainted as he
was with Caesar, with Memmius, with Lucretius, and
with the Roman literary circles. We have a short epigram
of Catullus (102) that might indicate that Nepos (whom
he here addresses by the vocative "Corneli" as in his
first poem) has told him under seal of secrecy of the
changed dedication and his part in it. Catullus assures
him that his secret will be forever safe. The awkward
phrasing of the verses so unusual for Catullus suggests
haste in composition:

> Si quicquam tacito commissum est fido ab amico
> Cuius sit penitus nota fides animi,
> Meque esse invenies illorum iure sacratum,
> Corneli, et factum me esse puta Harpocratem.[20b]

[b] "If anything has been confided by a trusted friend to a silent

So the *De Rerum Natura* came out dedicated to Memmius and with few knowing that he replaced Caesar. It may be that Virgil was one of the few who had heard of it, unless it is only by coincidence that Mnestheus, the mythical ancestor of Memmius, regularly came out second best in the contests of *Aeneid* v.

Books I, II, and v, generally regarded as the first to be finished, are those in which the name of Memmius occurs. Thus it appears that Lucretius began by addressing the object of his dedication directly by name occasionally but ceased to do so in Books III, IV, and VI, though there are many places in which he used the second person singular and speaks to him or to the "general reader." An invented patronymic "Memmiadae" (1.26) when the dedication to Caesar had to be abandoned, probably replaced an original "Aeneadae" (which would pick up the opening word of the whole work, "Aeneadum"). Memmius appears again in line 42 ("Memmi clara propago"). The context of both these mentions of Memmius seems better suited to Caesar than to Memmius, whose military career had not been impressive, though it must have justified the title of *imperator* on coins.[21]

Memmiadae (Aeneadae) nostro, quem tu, dea, tempore
   in omni   1.26
omnibus ornatum voluisti excellere rebus.[c]

In 1.41-43 there is a similar substitution:

---

one whose true heart is known through and through, you will find that I also am bound by their sacred law, Cornelius, and consider that I have become Harpocrates."

  [c] "for the son of the Memmii (Aeneadae), my friend, whom thou, goddess, through all his life hast wished to be adorned with every grace beyond his fellows."

nam neque nos agere hoc patriai tempore iniquo
possumus aequo animo nec Memmi clara propago
talibus in rebus communi desse saluti.[d]

However, since the genitive of Caesar is here metrically impossible, the gentile name would stand instead in "Juli clara propago."

Scholars have racked their brains to find a military crisis that Memmius might be called upon to handle, but so far have found nothing satisfactory[22] to explain the large scale operations described in II.40-46 and 323-32. Caesar's campaigns in the Gallic wars, however, would have seemed to a Transpadane like Lucretius overwhelming in their importance. All the people in the valley had seen and heard his legions marching and his annual cavalry recruitments. Some of his glory has lingered on to cling accidentally to the name of his successor in the dedication.

There are nine other places in Books I, II, and V where Memmius is addressed by name.[23] Since the vocatives *Caesar* and *Memmi* are metrically equivalent, it was fatally easy to substitute one for the other without attention to the context. Most of the lines are convincing for the name Caesar partly because its initial continues the series of repeated sounds that Lucretius seems to like. Book II.143 reads:

corporibus, paucis licet hinc cognoscere, Caesar.

Other cases where *Caesar* has the advantage over *Memmi* in sound are v.8, 93, 164, 1281f.[24] With v.867 it is the

[d] "for neither can we in our country's time of trouble pursue this task with untroubled mind, nor under such conditions can the noble offshoot of the Memmii (Caesars) neglect the public safety."

preceding line that carries the repetition, but *Caesar* is still effective:

lanigeraeque simul pecudes et bucera saecla.　　866
omnia sunt hominum tutelae tradita, Caesar.ᵉ

Many things point to a hasty and unfinished revision. Some of the remarks addressed to Memmius are far more pertinent to Caesar's vigorous and decided mind and achievements. Memmius himself was not without intelligence and ability to speak and write, but he was too lazy and self-indulgent to make the most of his capacity.²⁵ The opening appeal to Venus has no relation to Memmius, who did not share Caesar's divine ancestry. Difficulties occur where lines clearly referring to Caesar and no one else have been deleted, but there are *lacunae* where the transitions to the substituted verses were never completed. The most conspicuous of these breaks occur before and after Book 1.44-49, where a block of lines was transferred from II.646-51. It concerns the perfect existence of the gods and their detachment from the affairs of men. It seems now to stand as an interruption in the opening hymn to Venus, but the content would make it possible for the poet to have fused it into its context if he had not been interrupted in his revision.²⁶

In cases where the second person singular occurs without mention of a name it is impossible to be sure sometimes whether the author is speaking to his sponsor or to the "general reader." There are a number of such instances in Books I, II, and V, and even more in III, IV, and VI, where the name of Memmius does not occur at all. Some of the instances concerning only single words, such as the imperatives of *credo*, *video*, or *concipio*, are paren-

ᵉ "and withal the fleecy flocks and the horned herds are all trusted to the tutelage of men, Caesar." Bailey, modified.

thetical, and have as little effect on the sound of the verses
or the advancement of the argument as the common in-
troductory phrase "Nunc age." Others develop into considerable exhortations or arguments with a tone more or
less suited to Caesar or to Memmius. One such is near
the beginning of Book VI, where, after the opening praise
of Epicurus and his enlightening messages, we are
launched on a demonstration that when men fear divine interference in their affairs they are like children
frightened in the dark (VI.35-38):

> nam veluti pueri trepidant atque omnia caecis   35
> in tenebris metuunt, sic nos in luce timemus
> interdum, nilo quae sunt metucnda magis quam
> quae pueri in tenebris pavitant finguntque futura.[f]

Then he sums up what he has had to say about the mortal
structure of the universe and pronounces one of his peri-
odic demands for attention to the doctrine that is to
follow (VI.46):

> . . . quae restant percipe porro;

When confronted with the power of storms and tempests
men tend to stray back from true reason to the acceptance of old religious fears of divine masters. We return
to the object of this exhortation in the second person
(VI.68-79):

> quae nisi respuis ex animo longeque remittis
> dis indigna putare alienaque pacis eorum,
> delibata deum per te tibi numina sancta   70
> saepe oberunt; non quo violari summa deum vis

[f] "for even as children tremble and fear everything in blinding
darkness, so we sometimes dread in the light things that are no
whit more to be feared than what children shudder at in the
dark, and imagine will come to pass." Bailey.

possit, ut ex ira poenas petere imbibat acris,
sed quia tute tibi placida cum pace quietos
constitues magnos irarum volvere fluctus,
nec delubra deum placido cum pectore adibis,   75
nec de corpore quae sancto simulacra feruntur
in mentis hominum divinae nuntia formae,
suscipere haec animi tranquilla pace valevis.
inde videre licet qualis iam vita sequatur.ᵍ

This seems to be designed for Caesar, because it reflects
the reaction of Lucretius to his priestly connections.
After all, Caesar had been Pontifex Maximus since 63
B.C. (Plutarch, *J.C.* 13), and Lucretius, with his natural
honesty, could not imagine that any man could occupy
such a position without believing in the system of which
it was an essential part. Though Lucretius took a decided
stand against the orthodox establishment, he made obvious, though not always successful efforts to be tactful
about offense to Caesar's feeling.[27]

In Book III.417-20 we have another second-person passage that is too personal to refer to the "general reader"
and too complimentary for Memmius. Though it seems
that Lucretius had slight, if any, personal acquaintance

ᵍ "And unless you spew out all this from your mind and
banish far away thoughts unworthy of the gods and alien to
their peace, the holy powers of the gods, degraded by your
thought, will often do you harm; not that the high majesty of
the gods can be polluted by you, so that in wrath they should
yearn to seek sharp retribution, but because you yourself will
imagine that those tranquil beings in their placid peace set tossing
the great billows of wrath, nor with quiet breast will you approach the shrines of the gods, nor have strength to drink in
with tranquil peace of heart the images which are borne from
their holy body to herald their divine form to the minds of men.
And therefore what manner of life will follow, you may perceive."

with Memmius, it is hard to imagine his spending "happy toil" on shaping poetry worthy of the way of life of his intended convert.

> Nunc age, nativos animantibus et mortalis   III.417
> esse animos animasque levis ut noscere possis,
> conquisita diu dulcique reperta labore
> digna tua pergam disponere carmina vita.[h]

Nobody, on the other hand, could hesitate to deal with Memmius in the most downright and direct fashion, since there is no indication that he had any religious feeling. Doubtless in his official routines he had been required occasionally to participate in sacrifices and to take oaths in the name of the gods, but these ritual gestures had little meaning.

We do not know when Lucretius made the painful and difficult changes in his poem, but surely it was not before the official extension of Caesar's term in Gallia in 55 B.C. Lucretius probably continued to live in his Transpadane country and worked there on the last addition and revision of the *De Rerum Natura*. He probably had very little contact with Memmius, and the allusions to him in the poem do not show much understanding of his character.

Our complete ignorance about the close of the poet's life makes it uncertain how far the final experiences of Memmius could affect him. The candidacy for the consulship which promised to help the cause of Lucretius by keeping Memmius in the city actually caused his flight from Rome because of bribery scandals incidental to his

[h] "Come now, that you may be able to learn that the minds and the light souls of living things have birth and death, I will hasten to set forth verses long sought out and found with glad effort, worthy of your life."

campaign for the office in the winter of 55/54 B.C.[28] We have no reliable date for Lucretius's death, which most scholars conjecture to have occurred in 55. I incline to agree with Sandbach that 53 is more probable but largely because he had made considerable alterations in his work after the extension of Caesar's Gallic term in 55. So Lucretius probably lived to endure his second great frustration in the loss of Caesar's substitute for the dedication. He had certainly died, however, before 51 when Cicero wrote to Memmius the letter already mentioned in Chapter V.

Memmius, as we have seen, had chosen Athens for his life in exile and had happened to purchase the house of Epicurus. Naturally the Epicureans were deeply concerned to preserve their most sacred landmark and Cicero interceded with Memmius as they requested in spite of his contempt for their doctrines. There is no record of any reply from Memmius (if he ever troubled himself to make one) but it is assumed from what is known of his character that he would not be likely to inconvenience himself to spare the feelings of a troop of foolish Greeks. We do not know the fate of the house, but its new owner would not have hesitated to destroy it so that he might build a more suitable residence for himself. If so, he did not long enjoy it, for he died at Patras in 49 B.C.[29] Ironically enough, he may never have known of the honor paid to him by Lucretius.[30]

It was a bad moment in history for the appearance of a great poem when the *De Rerum Natura* was left in its still unfinished state. Rome was enduring the death of the Republic and the horrors of the power struggles that followed. Perhaps thanks to the accident that he too was a northerner, Virgil in his youth fell under the spell of Lucretius and Catullus and carried them in his mind and heart until he died. Reminiscences of both, but especially of Lucretius, recur throughout all his work. It was probably through Virgil's interest that both Catullus and Lucretius met what tardy recognition they both won in the age of Augustus. So it seems fitting that Virgil should have the last word. In spite of the frustrations which darkened his last days, Virgil's word for him is "felix" (*Georgics* II.490-93): "Happy was he who could understand the reasons for things, and put down under his feet all terrors and inexorable death and the roar of hungry Acheron." Centuries of familiarity and over-frequent quotation have not dulled the sonorous lines with their responsive echoes of Lucretian language:

> Felix qui potuit rerum cognoscere causas,
> Atque metus omnis et inexorabile fatum
> Subiecit pedibus strepitumque Acherontis avari.

Notes

CHAPTER I. *Regional Differences in Speech*
1. Cicero, *Brutus* 170f., 258; *De Oratore* III.41-45, especially 43 fin. Hendrickson, *C.P.* 12 (1917) 345.
2. From a learned Paduan I heard in my youth, Peter and Paul came to my ears as Petrus-uh et-uh Paulus-uh. It is well known that the speech of Apulia and Calabria differ widely from that of Emilia and Piedmont. Cf. Pelegrini, *forum italicum, Quarterly of Italian Studies*, State University of New York at Buffalo, 4 (1970) 231.
3. *The National Observer* of Jan. 11, 1975, quoting Harold Allen of the University of Minnesota. The *N. Y. Times* of February 17, 1972, p. 35, reports a project at the University of Wisconsin for a *Dictionary of American Regional English (DARE)*.
4. Salmon, *Samnium and the Samnites* 39. Cf. P. A. Brunt, *J.R.S.* 55 (1965) 18ff.
5. Salmon, "S.M.P.E." 12.
6. Quintilian, 1.5.56. See Duff, *Golden Age* 21.
7. Salmon, *Samnium and the Samnites* 275 with note 4; 343.
8. For regional speech, see Cicero, *Brutus* 172, echoed by Quintilian VIII.1.2.
9. Livy XXXVIII.36.7-9. See L. R. Taylor, *Voting Districts of the Roman Republic* 18; Salmon, *Samnium and the Samnites* 26, 194 with note 8, 250.
10. Cicero, *Brutus* 172. Catiline taunted Cicero with being an *inquilinus civis*: Sallust, *Catiline* 56.7.
11. Frank, *Catullus and Horace* 134; *idem, Vergil* 52, note 2; Tait, *Philodemus* 14f.
12. Duff, *Silver Age* 311ff.
13. Jerome, *Chron. Euseb.* under year 68.
14. Duff, *Silver Age* 329. On the severity of Messala as a critic, see Seneca, *Cont.* II.12.5: "Fuit autem Messala exactissimi

ingenii in omni studiorum parte, Latini sermonis observator diligentissimus." ["Messala was a man of most accurate mind in all branches of learning, a most scrupulous critic of the Latin language."] See above, page 7 for Messala's comment on Porcius Latro. Cf. also the famous charge of Patavinity which Pollio brought against Livy (Quintilian 1.5.56). For general comment on Pollio and Messala see Quintilian x.1.13.

15. Quintilian VIII.1.2.

16. In the work of the northern poets it is easy to find examples of their genius for sound effects. One notable instance is Virgil's *Aeneid* III.193: "caelum undique et undique pontus" (echoed in *Aeneid* v.8: "maria undique et undique caelum"), where the fleet is on the open sea with no land visible. In both passages *undae, undae* heave and swell across the scene as obviously as if they had been spelled out instead of being present only in the sound of *undique, undique* entirely unrelated in its dictionary meaning. Of course the elisions (surely pronounced) add to the motion we feel in the waves.

17. If Quintilian had noticed more of regional differences of sound and pronunciation, he might have contributed something more consistent and more helpful on one of the perennial problems in Latin, the sound of final *M*.

18. We must remember, however, that Quintilian's judgments on the poets are based not on aesthetic grounds but on suitability for quotation in speeches.

19. An obvious example of Horace's dependence on the meanings of the words he chooses rather than their sound or rhythm is the famous opening of the Soracte ode (I.9):

> Vides ut alta stet nive candidum
> Soracte, nec iam sustineant onus
> Silvae laborantes, geluque
> Flumina constiterint acuto.

["You see how Soracte stands white with deep snow, and the laboring woods no longer sustain their burden, and the streams have halted with sharp freezing."] As is usual with Horace, the choice of words is admirable. *Gelu acuto* (through their dictionary meanings only) vividly suggest not only the penetration of the cold but the effect of sudden freezing on shallow water flowing over sticks and stones, to be caught not in a smooth sheet but in jagged little peaks. The handling of the rhythm is a different matter. We can not feel that the very effective slowing of *silvae laborantes* is anything more than a happy accident of the Alcaic form he is following, when we come to the rhythmical ineptitude of the last line where the streams are halted stock still, in two galloping dactyls! The meaning of *constiterint* is perfect but does not suit its rhythm. As Havelock says (*Lyric Genius*, 182), Horace's odes are "exclusively a work of the intellect." Cf. Ferguson, *A.J.P.* 77 (1946) 13: "Horace moves the mind, Catullus the heart."

20. H. Last, *C.A.H.* IX.195; Robson, *C.J.* 29 (1933-34) 590-608.
21. Toynbee, *Hannibal's Legacy* II.184f.; Ewins, "Early Colonization of Cisalpine Gaul," *P.B.S.R.* 20 (1965) 62-71.
22. Frank, *Economic Survey of Ancient Rome* I.280; L. R. Taylor, *Voting Districts of the Roman Republic* 90f.
23. Strabo, V.I.II.
24. Cicero speaks in the *Pro Archia* 3.5 of better opportunities for study in the remoter places than in the capital.
25. Servius, *Commentarii* I init.; Wilkinson, *Georgics of Vergil* 201; Frank, *Vergil* 17.
26. Frank, *Vergil* 14, 17; Havelock, *Lyric Genius* 64; Baehrens, *Catulli Veronensis Liber* Part 2, Prolegomena, p. 24; Tait, *Philodemus* 14f.; Wiseman, *Cinna the Poet*.
27. The second marriage song (C. 62) had been included in an anthology and so has a special tradition in a codex known as T (Paris, 8071 S. IX). With this exception, the source of all that we know of Catullus's work is a codex known as V. V was lost soon after it was discovered in Verona in the fourteenth century, but fortunately had been copied before its disappearance. For a good account of the manuscript tradition see the preface of R.A.B. Mynors, *C. Valerii Catulli Carmina*, Oxford University Press, 1958.
28. *Catullus and Horace* 8; Whatmough, *Foundations of Roman Italy* 146ff.
29. For the survival of Gauls and Gallic culture, see Chevallier, "La celtique du Po," *Latomus* 21 (1962) 356-70.
30. For Gallic words, see Quintilian, 1.5.8 and 1.5.57. *Manni* is a word for horses, which Lucretius uses (III.1063) and which

Horace possibly borrows from him (*Odes* III.27.6; *Ep.* 1.7.77).
When Ovid uses the same word (*Amores* II.16.49): "rapien-
tibus esseda mannis," the word for the chariot that is being
whirled is also Gallic. Seneca (*Ep.* 87.10) lists *obesi manni*
with special breeds prized by luxury lovers (*asturco*,
"pacer," *tolutarius*, "trotter") in contrast to the old-fashioned Latin *equus* that old Cato rubbed down with his own
hands: "Ita non omnibus obesis mannis et asturconibus et
tolutariis praeferres unicam illum equum ab ipso Catone
defrictum."

31. It is interesting to see how much of the regionalism of Latin
reappears in Italian. Dante's use of elision sometimes seems
very close to Catullus: "La somma sapienza e il primo
amore," for instance, has his rippling breaks with every
syllable necessarily pronounced. The conjunction *e* would
otherwise be completely lost. Doubtless Dante could read
Virgil as Virgil intended.

32. *Brutus* 258; *De Oratore* III.42-45.

33. In *Pisonem* 53 and frags. 3 and 4.

34. *Ad Att.* VII.3.10; cf. *Brutus* 258.

35. *De Oratore* III.171ff.; *Orator* 150.

36. *Orator* 150 fin.

37. W. R. Hardie, *Res Metrica* 38f.: "generally avoided even in
prose," "kept within strict and well-defined limits."

38. Cicero in many places, e.g. *Orator* 162, 168, 173; *De Oratore*
III.196; *Brutus* 34 fin. See also Quintilian IX.4.116 and Aulus
Gellius XIII.21.1.

39. See, for example, Brooks Otis, *T.A.P.A.* 90 (1959) 167, for
connection of Scipio's dream in Cicero's *De Republica* with
Aeneid VI.

40. Cicero expresses a rather low opinion of poetry in general
(*De Rep.* IV.9; *Tusc. Dis.* II.27 and III.3; *N.D.* III.71. See
Thompson, *C.W.* 60 (1967) 230. J. F. D'Alton, *Roman
Literary Theory and Criticism* 149, says that for the most
part he "remained insensitive to the secret of the poetic
charm." Cf. Ellis, *Commentary on Catullus*, Prolegomena
XXII; Gordon Williams, *Tradition and Originality in Roman
Poetry* 721f.

41. *Orator* 152 fin.

42. *Brutus* 104, 211.

43. *De Partitione Oratoriae* 21: "—coniunctione quae neque asperos habeat concursus neque disiunctos atque hiantis." ["—by a combination of words that avoid both rough collisions (of consonants) and gaping juxtaposition of vowels." Rackham.]

44. See p. 13.

45. *Orator* 77: "Habet ille tamquam hiatus et concursus vocalium molle quiddam et quod indicet non ingratam neglegentiam de re hominis magis quam de verbis laborantis." ["—for the hiatus and clash of vowels has something agreeable about it and shows a not unpleasant carelessness on the part of a man who is paying more attention to the thought than to the words."Hubbell.]|

46. Soubiran, *L'élision* 607.

47. Elision is natural and avoidance of it is an artifice of poets (Sedgwick, *Mnemosyne* Ser. 4, 3 [1950] 67). Horace in the *Odes* shows extraordinary skill in fitting appropriate words into his rigidly fixed metrical schemes, and at the same time controlling the elision problem. On his word arrangement, see Commager, *The Odes of Horace* 50ff.; Wilkinson, *Golden Latin Artistry* 219. On his avoidance of elision, see Soubiran, *L'élision* 609. Wilkinson (*Ovid Recalled* 31) observes that elision is almost non-existent in Ovid.

48. Wilkinson, *Golden Latin Artistry* 85. See also M. Owen Lee, "Illustrative Elisions in Catullus," *T.A.P.A.* 93 (1962) 144-53. An example from Virgil is the passage cited below from *Eclogues* II.25f.

49. Ovid's mischievous delight in burlesquing Virgil's grave dignity by no means indicates a lack of appreciation. If Ovid had not absorbed Virgil as Virgil himself absorbed Lucretius, the frequently recurring flicks of parody and irreverent perversion of phrases would have been impossible. For examples of his parodies see B. Otis, *Ovid as an Epic Poet* 18, 96ff., 290.

50. As Jackson Knight observes (Herescu's *Ovidiana* 120) Ovid may regard elision as a convenience, but not as an instrument of art; his elisions are "rare and relatively light." This seems borne out by his borrowing from Catullus 76, 11f.:

> Quin tu animo affirmas atque istinc teque reducis
> et dis invitis desinis esse miser?

["Why do you not make up your mind and bring yourself back from that state and cease to be wretched against the will of the gods?"] He seems not to realize how Catullus by the application and the suspension of elision has pointed the shift from indecision to firm resolve, for he smooths away those effective breaks (*Met.* IX.745):

> Quin animum firmas teque ipsa recolligis, Iphi?

Modern ears differ as the ancients did. J. A. Richmond (*Atti del convegnio internazionale Ovidiano* II, 38f.) calls Ovid's changes "correcting the lapses of his predecessors." K. R. Harrington, *Roman Elegiac Poets* (edition of 1968), 66, notes that Ovid is the most careful of the elegists in avoiding elision as Catullus is the least. B. Otis, *Ovid as an Epic Poet* 75ff., quotes Siedow, *De Elisionis Usu* 55 to show that Ovid uses less than one third as many elisions in *Metamorphoses* as Virgil in the *Aeneid*.

51. The northern habit of eliding essential monosyllables suggests that they were pronounced, e.g. Lucretius 1.150: "nullam rem e nilo gigni divinitus umquam." ["that nothing is ever created from nothing by divine power."] For the treatment of monosyllables, see J. Hellegouarc'h, *Le monosyllabe dans l'hexamètre latine*, Paris (1964).

52. Propertius II.34.66f. Propertius uses more elisions than Tibullus or any Augustan except Virgil and more even than Virgil in the *Eclogues*. See Soubiran, *L'élision* 249, 605; Platnauer, *Latin Elegiac Verse* 73 with note 1.

53. Horace outlived Virgil by more than a decade and had ample opportunity to allude to his later works, but he never refers to anything later than the *Eclogues*. To those he applied the casual and somewhat enigmatic "molle atque facetum" (*Satires* 1.10.43f.), which has been endlessly discussed. Horace may have been remembering the "molle quiddam" which Cicero (*Orator* 77) uses, of writing marked by many open junctions, a feature that Horace doubtless disliked in Virgil's verse (see note 49, above, and related text). Even that slight notice has seemed to indicate more a feeling of friendship than any "native sympathy" for the work. See T. Frank, *Vergil* 147 and Jackson Knight, *Roman*

Vergil 49. It is remarkable that Horace never mentions Virgil's death or expresses a word of regret for the loss of one he had called "animae dimidium meae" (*Odes* 1.3.8).

54. Kent and Sturtevant (*T.A.P.A.* 46 [1921] 124ff.) advocate complete suppression of the elided syllable. W. S. Allen, *Vox Latina*, agrees with them. Soubiran, *L'élision* 614, 648, takes the opposite view. Hardie, *Res Metrica*, Appendix p. 265, also maintains, "The vowel did not count metrically, though it is not to be supposed that it was altogether inaudible or entirely omitted by the voice."

55. The phrase and the idea recur in histories and commentaries, e.g. Paratore and Pizzani, *Lucreti De Rerum Natura*, "congiura del silenzio"; DeWitt, *Roman Epicureanism* Section 2, p. 34; W. F. Jackson Knight, *Roman Vergil* 45.

56. "Horace and Valerius Cato," *C.P.* 12 (1917) 345.

CHAPTER II. *Catullus: Northern Characteristics*

1. *Lives of the Caesars*, "Divus Julius" 73: "Valerium Catullum, a quo sibi versiculis de Mamurra perpetua stigmata imposita non dissimulaverat, satisfacientem eodem die adhibuit cenae hospitioque patris eius, sicut consuerat, uti perseveravit." ["When Valerius Catullus had made suitable apology, though Caesar did not disguise his feeling that a lasting stain had been left upon his name by the verses against Mamurra, he invited Catullus to dinner the same day and continued to make use of his father's hospitality as had been his custom."] Suetonius clearly indicates a host-guest relationship of some duration.

2. See Chapter I, p. 13.

3. To entertain Caesar was probably no light assignment, though less burdensome in his proconsular days than in 45 B.C., when Cicero suffered a visit from the dictator and his retinue (*Ad Att.* XIII.52.2): "Hospes tamen non is quoi diceres, 'Amabo te, eodem ad me cum reverteres.' Semel satis est." ["Still he was not the kind of guest to whom one would say, 'Do by all means drop in on your way back.' Once is enough."] Besides the military escort encamped in the fields, there were not only a costly dinner for Caesar

himself but entertainment for his aides in three dining
rooms, and suitable provision elsewhere for freedmen and
slaves.

4. Varus, a close friend of Catullus (10) is already a respected
judge of poetry. He lived to be a distinguished figure in the
literary circles of Augustan Rome. That Virgil mourned his
death we know from Horace, *Odes* 1.24. In the *Ars Poetica*
438ff., Horace speaks of him as an authority. Virgil probably
went through "the same curriculum as Catullus and the
older Transpadane poets and was familiar with the 'roll of
honor' at the school" in Cremona (Tait, *Philodemus* 53).

5. Catullus 50. Calvus is the only one of the *poetae novi* known
to us who was not a northerner (Havelock, *Lyric Genius*
64), but a member of an old Roman plebeian family. The
few surviving fragments of his verse show metrical forms
used also by Catullus, and the two are frequently mentioned
together (Horace, *Sat.* 1.10.19; Ovid, *Am.* III.9.61f.; Aulus
Gellius, XIX.9.7; Pliny, *Ep.* 1.16.5). It is hard to believe that
such an intimate association sprang up only after Catullus
went to Rome and in spite of the absorbing affair with
Lesbia, who did not number Calvus among her cronies. We
do not know who the mother of Calvus was, or in what
province his father was serving when the charge of extortion
was brought against him. It is tempting to conjecture that
after the father's tragic death when Calvus was sixteen his
mother and he went north to escape the gossip of the capital
for a time and that there a schoolboy friendship with Catullus might have been formed. (For the trial and conviction
of his father see E. S. Gruen, *H.S.C.P.* 71 [1967] 215-34.)
Like Catullus, Calvus had written lampoons about Caesar
(Suetonius, "Divus Julius," 73).

6. His prominent father was probably an officeholder and so
would be a Roman citizen (Frank, *Catullus and Horace*
4ff.). For the general extension of citizenship to Gallia
Cisalpina, see *C.A.H.* IX.643.

7. By the time he wrote 11.9-12, Catullus had evidently re-
nounced his hostility to Caesar.

8. For the manuscript tradition see Mynors, *C. Valerii Catulli
Carmina, Praefatio.*

9. Calvus is of course an exception, but Cicero discusses him

as an orator, not as a poet (*Brutus* 283ff.; *Ad Fam.* xv.21.4). The others are called *"poetae novi"* (*Orator* 161); "Cantores Euphorionis" (*Tusc.* III.19.45); "νεώτεροι" (*Ad Att.* VII.2.1).

10. *Phoenix* 12 (1968) 106.

11. *Lyric Genius* 112.

12. T. Frank, *A.J.P.* 40 (1919) 409. R. Ellis, *Commentary on Catullus* 2nd ed. (1889) 169f., sums up opinions in his time. For later interpretations, see Worrell, *Phoenix* 17 (1963) 159f.; Havelock, *Lyric Genius* 96; Fordyce, *Catullus, A Commentary* 213f.; Laughton, *C.P.* 66 (1971) 36; Thomson, *C.W.* 60 (1967) 225-30. All interpretations are unfortunately subjective.

13. For discussion of the theme, see H. B. Rosen, *Mnemosyne* Ser. 4, 14 (1969) 224-32; L'Enchantin de Gubernatis, *Riv. Fil.* 40 (1920) 444-48; D. Braga, *Catullo e i Poeti Greci*, Messina and Florence 1950, 227ff.

14. Cicero mentions the departure of Crassus in a letter to Lentulus, written from Rome in 54 B.C. (*Ad Fam.* I.9.20): "Paene a meis laribus in provinciam est profectus, nam cenavit apud me in mei generi Crassipedis hortis." ["He set out for the province almost from my household, for he had dined with me in the gardens of my son-in-law Crassipedes."] After their public reconciliation, Cicero continues to express in private feelings anything but friendly toward Crassus. He writes to Atticus (IV.13.2) after a word about the departure, "O hominem nequam!"

15. E.g. Ellis, *Commentary on Catullus* 459f.; Fordyce, *Commentary* on 84.5f.; Quinn, *Catullus*, note on 84.5f.

16. For the date of the *De Oratore*, see Wilkins' edition, introduction, 2f.

17. For the word *pressu*, see Chapter I, note 43 with related text. Cicero contrasts *presse* (used for the neatly closed mouth) with *hiulce* and *vaste* for the open-mouthed effect of the open vowel junctions.

18. See *Ad Att.* II.14.2 and 15.3 for Cicero's difficulties with Arrius as a neighbor at Formiae. Cicero meditates a retreat to Arpinum to escape his unwelcome visits. Cf. Ramage, *C.P.* 54 (1959) 44ff.

19. According to D. M. Jones, *P.C.A.* 53 (1956) 26, the exaggerated aspirates are plebeian but not non-Roman.

20. Because of a feeling that servile origin is inappropriate for Arrius, *umber* has been proposed as an emendation for *liber* in line 5 (Hermann, *Latomus* 16 [1959] 681, following Riese). This has not been generally accepted. It is not necessary to debate the literal truth of anything Catullus alleges about Arrius and his kin. The chief point of the epigram is to parody Cicero's annoying claims about Laelia and Roman perfections. With no fear of libel laws, Catullus is free to fill out his picture with any details he thinks will make it more effective.

21. See above, note 14.

22. E. S. Gruen, *H.S.C.P.* 71 (1967) 226.

23. See Chapter I, p. 15.

24. *T.A.P.A.* 93 (1962) 145. If it is true, as I believe the evidence shows, that elided syllables were pronounced in the verse of Catullus and his *conterranei*, then final *M* should also retain its sound value, since *M* with the vowel before it was elided like a vowel.

25. D. A. West, *C.Q.* N.S. 7 (1957) 102.

26. Wilkinson, *Golden Latin Artistry* 55 note, cites the scorching comments of Ellis, Knoll, Herescu, and Knobbe. Though Catullus 73.6 has been called the most heavily elided line in Latin, it is surpassed by a line of Caecilius Statius which Cicero quotes in *De Senectute* 25: "Sentire ea aetate eumpse esse odiosum alteri," in which all seven words are elided. (Caecilius is also a Transpadane.) See Oldfather, *C.J.* 38 (1942-43) 479. See above, Chapter I, p. 13.

27. D. A. West, *C.Q.* N.S. 7 (1957) 102; Wilkinson, *Golden Latin Artistry* 55; Owen Lee, *T.A.P.A.* 93 (1962) 132; Ferguson, *A.J.P.* 81 (1960) 339.

28. Ross, *Style and Tradition in Catullus* 126, cites from Catullus four other examples of elision at the diaeresis of the pentameter: 88.6 (nympharum), 68.10 (musarum), 69.90 (virtutum), 90.4 (Persarum), but does not note that all are elisions of *um*. The only Augustan examples are both from Propertius (1.5.32; III(1-),22.10), who as usual is aligned with the northern poets.

29. *Golden Latin Artistry* Chapter III.

30. See above, note 24 and Chapter I, p. 18.

31. J. Soubiran, *L'élision*.

32. Keil, *Grammatici Latini* II.29 for Priscian Book I, part 2. Of course we have no idea how the phrases *multum ille* and *quantum erat* sounded as commonly pronounced in Quintilian's time, and so the illustration is meaningless to us, as are Priscian's examples.

33. E. Diehl, "De *M* finali epigraphica"; E. H. Sturtevant, *The Pronunciation of Greek and Latin*, 2nd ed., Philadelphia 1940, 153; Niedermann, *Précis de phonétique du Latin*, 146.

34. Velius Longus (Keil, VII.80.18) records that Verrius Flaccus used a half *M* (Λ), Cato the Elder apparently used an *M* turned on its side, which Quintilian (IX.4.39) mistook for an *E*. See Kent, *Sounds of Latin* 38, par. 19.

35. *Précis de phonétique du Latin* 149.

36. Duff translates: "beslobbers, embraces, and devours one with affection," *Golden Age* 178.

37. "Catullus and Ovid," *A.J.P.* 81 (1960) 337.

38. For the question of eliding words ending in *M* (quasi-cretics), see edition Bailey 1.120, Prolegomena VI.14.5. The Augustans in general avoided this practice, but it is not rare in Catullus, Lucretius, and Virgil. The latter regularly avails himself of it with *Ilium*, which otherwise could not be used in hexameter verse.

39. On the difference of Propertius from Tibullus and Ovid, see Wilkinson, *Golden Latin Artistry* 85, notes 133, 134; *Ovid Recalled* 35. Platnauer, *Latin Elegiac Verse* 73, calls Propertius least careful of the elegists in avoiding elision. Cf. Steele, *P.Q.* 8 (1951) 50. Soubiran, *L'élision* 249, notes that Propertius differs from Tibullus in treatment of final *M*; 605, after Virgil the use of elision declined except for Propertius who uses more than occur in the *Eclogues*. Propertius has occasional spondaic endings in his hexameters, while Tibullus has none whatever and Ovid very few in all his extensive text; Catullus uses only two spondaic hexameters in his elegiacs, but uses them more frequently in hexameters of 64. Cf. Platnauer, *Latin Elegiac Verse* 38f.

40. Elder, *H.S.C.P.* 60 (1961) 120.

41. Elder, *H.S.C.P.* 60 (1961) 115.

42. Lucretius II.27 couples *renidet* with *fulget* to describe the shining splendor of a rich house.

43. Martial and Statius furnish the only texts we have besides

Catullus's which make extensive use of hendecasyllables. They depart from the freedom of Catullus in varying the opening foot and in the use of elision, which is either avoided completely or rarely admitted. Even Martial, for all his cleverness, is far inferior to Catullus in "expressiveness." There are, however, those who admire smooth uniformity and censure Catullus as "duriusculus." See Garrod, "Elision in Hendecasyllables" 90-94.
44. Havelock, *Lyric Genius* 6. Cf. also Hack, *H.S.C.P.* 25 (1914) 111f.

CHAPTER III. *Lucretius: Northern Linguistics*

1. See Chapter II above.
2. E.g., Cyril Bailey, *Titi Lucreti Cari, De Rerum Natura*, Oxford (1947), I.1-21; F. H. Sandbach, *C.R.* 54 (1940) 12ff.; H.A.J. Munro, *T. Lucreti Cari, De Rerum Natura*, Cambridge Press 4th edition (1893) II.1ff.
3. Catullus 116.8: "at fixus nostris tu *dabis supplicium*." ["But pierced by my weapons you will pay the penalty."] This happens to be the very end of the Catullus book, but the poems are not in chronological order. In fact, Merrill (*Catullus*, Introduction 72) considers this the earliest of the seven Gellius epigrams. Cicero (*Orator* 161) tells us that the practice, though unquestioned in earlier writing, was avoided by the *poetae novi* as "rather countrified" (*subrusticum*). For the Lucretian use see Bailey, Proleg. VI.10, pp. 123ff.
4. Sikes, *Lucretius, Poet and Philosopher* 39; see also Gordon Williams, *Tradition and Originality in Roman Poetry* 716f.
5. Aim of Lucretius, I.50-61; praise of Epicurus, I.62-79; III.1-13; V.1-13.
6. Cicero returns repeatedly to criticism of over-elided provincial speech (which he calls *vastus, hians, hiulcus*) as opposed to the neater diction ("ipso oris pressu") of Roman *urbanitas*. E.g. *De Oratore* III.43, 45, 172. See also above, Chapter I, pp. 13-4 and Chapter II on the Arrius poem, pp. 25-6.
7. Elision of monosyllables, for instance, is common enough

not only in Lucretius and Catullus but in Virgil, who shares and continues so many of their regional speech habits. For the special treatment of *est* (enclisis or aphaeresis) see Soubiran, *L'élision* 159-84. The elision of *sum* in Lucretius v.337, "nunc ego sum in patrias qui possim vertere voces," Merrill calls "harsh but permissible" in his note on the line. It occurs also in Virgil, *Eclogues* II.25, "non sum adeo informis." Cicero admits three cases, involving only two pronouns (*te* once and *se* twice). These might be written *t'* and *s'* and could hardly disturb the most determined opponent of elision. Lucretius elides *tu, mi, si, quo, quae, re, vi, cum, dum, sum, rem, vim*, words that often, as essential to the meaning, must be fully pronounced. See Merrill, *U. of Cal. Stud. Cl. Phil.* 7 (1924) 301. Cf. also Deutsch, *Pattern of Sound* 158ff.

8. On the question of pronunciation of elided syllables, see W. R. Hardie, *Res Metrica* 39; Soubiran, *L'élision* 55ff. Wilkinson, *Golden Latin Artistry* 133f., makes much of Augustan departure from Catullan types of elision, but while his remarks apply to Tibullus and Ovid, they do not apply to Virgil who continues his northern habits into his work on the *Aeneid*. Cf. testimony of Valerius Probus in Aulus Gellius 13.21.6, where it is important to decide between *turrim* and *turrem* in *Aeneid* II.460, though the crucial final syllable is elided before "in praecipiti." For examples of elided monosyllables which must be pronounced, see *Aeneid* I.219 (*iam*) and 1.308 (*nam*).

9. See above, Chapter II, p. 33.

10. See above, Chapter II, p. 33.

11. This is a good example of a final *M* that the context clearly requires should be fully pronounced.

12. Virgil makes use of the elision but also far surpasses Lucretius in using the caesura for a similar purpose.

13. Leonard and Smith, 200, note on Lucretius 1.13.

14. *C.P.* 12 (1917) 341.

15. 1.219, cf. edition Ernout, Introduction 44, "élisions et hiatus pénibles."

16. Leonard and Smith, 159 with note 9 where these examples are cited for "excessive elision": 1.234; II.248; III.793; IV.618,

741; v.547. It is surprising to find iv.618 in this list since it contains only two elisions, and the sound pattern is strikingly effective for descriptive purposes:

> mandendo expremimus, ceu plenam spongiam aquai.

It does, however, show one of the "quasi-cretic" elisions (*spongiam aquai*) which scholars consider abnormal though it occurs not only in Lucretius and Catullus but in Virgil regularly with the name "Ilium." See edition Bailey, I, Prolegomena vi.14.5, p. 129.

17. See Munro's note on Lucretius iv.741, where he also notes a general opinion that the elision of *equi atque* is intolerably harsh. Leonard and Smith, 588, in a note on this same line iv.741 make a direct comparison with Catullus 73.6.
18. Compare similar contrast in Catullus, Chapter II above, pp. 38-9.
19. See above, Chapter II, pp. 38-9.
20. C.Q., N.S. 7 (1957) 98-102.
21. *Fatendumst* is not in effect an elision since the aphaeresis of *est* makes no metrical change in the line.
22. Soubiran, *L'élision* 622ff., recognizes the use of broken and unbroken rhythms in an argument. For examples of un-elided statements which appear intermittently in Lucretius see i.248f., 304, 548; ii.79, 99ff., 105, 180ff.; iii.970. There are scores of examples in all the books except vi, which shows less of this kind of contrast.
23. See Chapter II, pp. 41-2.
24. Deutsch, *Pattern of Sound*, devotes most of her study to his various uses of repetition. A good summary of Lucretius's uses of repetitions in Bailey 1.144f. For repetition of unusual words, p. 145.
25. To our knowledge the word is not used before Lucretius.
26. It has apparently no exact equivalent in Latin, since *spurius* is more limited in its range.
27. Grammarians use *nothus* for borrowed Greek names declined with Latin endings (Varro, *L.L.* 10.69). In Catullus 63.27 Attis, as neither man nor woman, is called "notha mulier."
28. Bailey's "pool of water" gives the result but has lost the process.

29. Surely it was not the busy river port of Ostia as some have suggested. It might be some retired cove on the upper Adriatic or one of the less frequented beaches of Campania or Etruria.
30. Cf. 1.251.
31. Leonard and Smith, usually most perceptive, have a strange note on "breakers" with enough "weight and momentum" to "beat" the beach. Only a violent storm certainly not suggested in "mollibus undis" could account for such an uproar.
32. See Bailey's note on II.376.
33. Virgil feels the full impact of Lucretian phrases and the cadences, permanently stored away in his mind, reappear throughout his work, but usually in contexts with no relation to the original. Thus he uses *bibula harena* in drawing off the excess moisture of a swampy place (*Georgics* 1.227) and in that same passage with *collectum umorem* he recalls *collectus aquae* of Lucretius IV.414. Also in *Aeneid* VI.227 we find *bibulam favillam* where the ashes of the funeral pyre drink up the wine of the libation. A still different association comes with the preparation of porous soil for newly planted cuttings: "aut lapidem bibulum aut squalentis infode" where the shells are an additional reminder of "concharum," Lucretius II.374. Horace, on the other hand, to whom sound means less, may repeat the idea of Lucretius with none of his words. Cf. Horace *Odes* 1.3.21ff.:

> nequiquam deus abscidit
> prudens oceano dissociabili
> terras—

Cf. Lucretius V.203:

> et mare quod late terrarum distinet oras.

34. See above, note 33.
35. This secondary reminiscence (*rigor auri*) is separated from the *serra* passage in Lucretius by a whole book length. This is one of many indications that Virgil has in his mind the entire work and not just occasional striking phrases.
36. Jackson Knight, *Poetic Inspiration* 40.

37. Virgil uses the simple verb *angit* for the strangling of Cacus in *Aen.* VIII.260 and for his animal plague in *Georgics* III.497.
38. On Lucretian inventions, Bailey, Proleg. 1.137f. See Aulus Gellius, *N.A.* 1.21.5 for Virgil's use of *amaror*. Some editors read *amaro* in *Georgics* II.247.
39. *Poetic Inspiration* 45.
40. Edition Ernout, Introduction 2.
41. Especially Horace and Ovid.

CHAPTER IV. *Lucretius: Northern Landscape and Culture*

1. In favor of Roman birth e.g. are Merrill, Introduction 14ff.; Bailey 1.5; Munro, II.1ff.; Duff, *Golden Age* 205: "It was probable that Lucretius, like Caesar, was a native of Rome."
2. For northern birth, Marx, *Neue Jahrbücher* 3 (1899) 532- 48; Mewaldt, *R.E.* XIII.1659ff.; Regenbogen, *Lukrez* 19.
3. Chapter III, pp. 46-7.
4. Chapter III, pp. 48ff.
5. For a summary of Graeco-Roman factors see Merrill 14 and Bailey 1.4.
6. 1.315.
7. M. Bieber, *Greek and Roman Theatre* 79, 157ff.
8. Pliny, *N.H.* 19.23. Cf. Williams, *Tradition and Originality* 663ff., with good discussion of the Lucretius passage.
9. Remains of theaters in the Po valley in Ventimiglia, Milano, Brescia, and Aosta. There has never been a thorough examination of the theater at Verona to find if there was a pre-Augustan building on the site, but it is quite possible that Verona had a permanent theater long before Rome, which was one of the last important places to acquire one, Pompey's theater, 55 B.C.
10. IV.979ff. Cf. L. R. Taylor, *Phoenix* Suppl. 1.147-151.
11. Probably before he became *curule aedile* in 65 B.C. See Gelzer's *Caesar*, Zeittafel. Suetonius, "Divus Julius" (x.2), says Caesar had so many gladiators on hand when aedile that his opponents felt a law was needed to limit numbers.
12. Bailey, note on II.323, expresses some doubt that this passage refers to the Campus Martius, though he accepts that identification for II.40f. For Lucretius's use of *campus* in

general sense: III.1002 "petit aequora campi" of the stone of Sisyphus, and other examples in V.492 and VI.712, 736.

13. III.1029ff.

14. Bailey, I. Proleg. p. 14; Gelzer (tr. by Needham), *Caesar* 17.

15. He does not mention the Tiber by name, and the flooded river he describes (I.288f.) does not suit the Tiber, which has no *grandia saxa* in its muddy course. Floods bring down trees, fragments of buildings, etc., but no rocks. He does name the Nile (VI.712).

16. An allusion to the geese that saved the *arx* (IV.683), and earlier to the punishments associated with the unnamed Capitoline Hill (III.1016f.) depend on book knowledge, not personal experience.

17. Besides Mars and Venus, there are Jupiter, Neptune, Ceres, Liber, Bacchus, Pan, Hercules, and others.

18. I.77, 596 ("alte terminus haerens"); II.1087; III.1020; V.90; VI.66. The last two cases seem clearly metaphorical but the others may refer to Terminus as a god.

19. Lucretius does not mention some details which we learn from others, chiefly Ovid *Met.* II.1-367. Catullus, 64.290f. and Virgil *Aen.* X.189f. refer to the story allusively.

20. Ovid, *Fasti* IV.341ff. After landing at the junction of the Almo and the Tiber, the goddess entered Rome by the Porta Capena, in an ox-drawn cart and proceeded to her temple on the Palatine.

21. We must keep in mind the sometimes neglected fact that the whole Magna Mater passage (II.598ff.) is introduced as an image or symbol of the idea that earth is called the mother of men and crops and beasts because it contains all the elements from which life is produced and sustained.

22. T.R.S. Broughton, *Historia* 2 (1953) 209-212 discusses the help she gave to Marius against the Cimbri in 102 B.C. His thank offerings to her may have helped to establish her prominence in the region. For the Cisalpine cult of Cybele see also Pascal, *Coll. Latomus* 75, 158 and Colin, "Megalesia," *Athenaeum* N.S. 32 (1954) 341.

23. Pascal, *Coll. Latomus* 75, 189ff.

24. O. Tescari, *Lucrezio*, Rome 1939, 9.

25. Leonard and Smith 20.
26. He has several notes on effects only to be seen from on board a boat and not from the land (iv.387-90). There is no evidence that he ever sailed as far as Greece, as he might well have done as a student of philosophy.
27. Cf. the relatively feeble effort of Horace's Soracte ode (1.9):

> geluque
> flumina constiterunt acuto.

Cicero has a good passage in *De Natura Deorum* 2.26 that may be taken from Lucretius: "neque nive pruina concresceretur."
28. *Duramen* may be one of his inventions. See Bailey 1. Proleg. VII.2.
29. Rosamund Deutsch is an exception. She comments on the contrast (*Pattern of Sound* 16) between "crisp frost" and "softly falling snow." She recognizes the effectiveness of lines 20 and 21, gets the sound, but misses the motion.
30. Bailey translates *violat* by the violently ugly word "besmirch." We can not censure his failure, because Lucretius is not translatable. The poet has used the right words and to substitute other words is to destroy what he has made. Not only sound and rhythm but breaks between words, and motion suggested but not stated are all essential. Here *acri* means both that the crystal has a cutting edge that the cold of the frosty *pruina* is biting. *Concreta* "grown together" as here applied became commonplace after Lucretius but here carries an interesting suggestion of the union of many elements in a complex structure. Lucretius often is less concerned with a passive state than with the process that produced it.
31. W. E. Leonard has a good summary of the places in his essay in edition Leonard and Smith 18f.
32. Lucretius II.196-200.

CHAPTER V. *Nepos and Cicero*

1. As usual with provincials of his time, the birthplace of Nepos and the dates of his birth and death are not recorded

in our sources. The elder Pliny's remark (*N.H.* III.127) that
he was "Padi accola," "a dweller near the Po," does not
indicate which side of the river, but I know of no modern
scholar who does not regard Nepos as a Transpadane. His
close connection with Catullus (e.g. Catullus 1.3-7) suggests
he was a northerner. A good summary of the clues leading
to the inference that Nepos came from the Insubrian town
of Tianum (between Mediolanum and the Po) is in Duff,
Golden Age 309 with note 5.

2. This one sentence is enough to show the awkward style of
Nepos. We can understand the embarrassment of Catullus
in his attempt in the first poem to allude politely to his
history without misrepresenting the facts. In "Doctis, Iup-
piter, et laboriosis" (line 7) he says the books are learned
and show hard work spent on them, but says nothing about
the quality of the result.

3. *Ad Q. Fr.* II.10(9), edition Tyrrell and Purser, no. 132. The
numbering of the letters in the second book of *Ad Q. Fr.* is
confused by the division of no. 4 by modern scholars, so the
Lucretius letter is variously numbered as 9, 10, or 11 in different editions. I use Sjögren's numbers (*M. Tulli Ciceronis ad Q. Fratrem Epistolarum, Libri tres*) for this (10)
and the second (11) and third (12) of the series.

4. See Chapter VI, pp. 106f.

5. Paratore, *Introd.* 16; De Witt, *Roman Epicureanism* 39.

6. Jackson Knight, *Poetic Inspiration* 45. U. Pizzani (*Il pro-
blema del testo e della composizione del De rerum natura di
Lucrezio*, Rome 1959, 46) insists that Lucretius was well-
known in Rome because he was known to Catullus and
Nepos, but he ignores the geographical factor.

7. *Ad Q. Fr.* II.10(9).

8. *Ad Att.* III.9; III.10; III.13 fin.; III.17 fin.; III.19 fin.; esp.
III.23 fin. All the letters of this book are full of allusions to
Quintus and Marcus's worry about him.

9. "Epistulam hanc convicio efflagitarunt codicilli tui." Evidently Quintus is displaying the traits against which his
brother warned him in *Ad Q. Fr.* 1.1.37f., *iracundia* and
acerbitas; 38 "quotidie meditere resistendum esse iracun-
diae"; 39 "vehementiores animi concitationes."

10. For the impatient letter carrier, see *Ad Fam.* XV.17.1; XV.18.1.

Notes to Chapter V

11. Another letter (*Ad Att.* II.20.6) refers to a poet, but is cryptic enough to be one of those code messages Cicero warns his friend to expect when plain statements in writing seem too dangerous. (*Ad Att.* II.19 fin., II.20: "A Vibio libros accepi. Poeta (not Vibius but the man whose writings he had lent to Cicero) ineptus est et tamen scit nihil, sed est non inutilis." The un-named man is stupid, but may be useful for the very reason that he does not understand what is going on.

12. See Cicero's next letter (*Ad Q. Fr.* II.12, edition Tyrrell and Purser, 134): "Risi 'nivem atram' teque hilari animo esse et prompto ad iucundum valde me iuvat." ["I laughed at your 'black snow' and I am delighted that you are in a cheerful mood and ready to crack a joke."]

13. See Sandbach, *C.R.* 54 (1940) 75; Brink, *Horace on Poetry*, Cambridge 1963, 62 with note 5. *Poema* may be *pars parva* of long work or a short piece.

14. For the observation that Cicero's remark is a hasty comment given too much attention, see Sihler, *T.A.P.A.* 28 (1897) 46, who calls it the "tag end of a hasty letter." Cf. Bignone, *Storia* II.163.

15. Jachmann, *Athenaeum* 45 (1967) 89-118; Paratore, *Rivista di cultura classica e medioevale* 2 (1960) 133, calls the terms "concetti e termine canonici." He accepts Traglia's suggestion on *multae artis* that Cicero feels the *ars* is excessive, being always present, while the *ingenium* appears in flashes (*lumina*).

16. Cicero denies to Memmius (*Ad Fam.* XIII.1) that Atticus is an Epicurean, but he is commonly said to be one. Other Epicurean friends of Cicero were Cassius (see below, p. 99) and Trebatius, who was one of the Epicurean group in Caesar's camp in Gaul. See Farrington, *Faith of Epicurus* 138.

17. Cicero, *Pro Sulla* 6.24; *De Fin.* II.74.

CHAPTER VI. *The Change of Dedication*

1. Leonard and Smith 20. Luc. 1.921-50 (repeated in IV.1-25) also alludes to his purpose. He is human enough to include a thought of personal recognition and lasting fame. (1.136-45

136

speaks of the difficult task "propter egestatem linguae," and the newness of the theme to express in Latin verses "Graiorum abscura reperta.")

2. Bockemüller and Kannengiesser both regarded Memmius as a second choice. See Bailey 1.32, note 5, and II, note on Luc. 1.50ff.

3. Gelzer, *Caesar* 28ff.; Taylor, *C.P.* 36 (1941) 122. A few special centers (e.g. the former Latin colonies of Cremona and Aquileia) already had the citizenship, as had also men in the Latin colonies who were elected to public office.

4. Gelzer, *Caesar* 28ff.; Taylor, *C.P.* 36 (1941) 123.

5. Suetonius, "Divus Julius," VI.

6. *Ad Fam.* VIII.15.2. The same letter (written in 49 B.C.) speaks of a *hospes* of Caesar from Gallia Cisalpina, an indication of the lasting bond between him and the Transpadanes. Velleius II.41.1 attests Caesar's descent. See Perret, *Origines de la Légende Troyenne de Rome*, Paris 1942, especially pp. 571ff.

7. Gelzer, *Caesar* 244.

8. *B.G.* V.I.I: "—descendens ab hibernis Caesar in Italiam ut quotannis facere consuerat." Cf. T. Rice Holmes, *Caesar's Conquest of Gaul*, Oxford 1911, 579-81.

9. Leonard and Smith 19; Bailey, I, Proleg. 1.4, p. 5. Traglia, while accepting the Campus Martius as the site, thought the troops were Caesar's men drilling before he went north.

10. For translation, see above, Chapter IV, note e.

11. For translation, see above, Chapter IV, note d.

12. See above, Chapter III, p. 50.

13. Suetonius, "Divus Julius," 73. The hostile poems of Catullus on Caesar are 29 and 57, both probably written in 55 B.C.

14. *Greece and Rome*, Ser. 2 (1958) 5, 181f. Dale suggests (p. 182) that Quintus Cicero might have carried a copy of the work when he went to join Caesar in Gaul.

15. Pompey's dedication to Venus Victrix in the theater shrine of 55 B.C. was too long past to enter into the decision.

16. Jerome's note on Eusebius says that Lucretius was driven mad by a love potion and committed suicide after composing the *De Rerum Natura* in lucid intervals. See Bailey I, Proleg. 5, pp. 8ff.

17. For the family tree of Memmius, see Wiseman, *C.Q.* 17

(1967) 64ff. Marx (*Neue Jahrbücher* 8 [1899] 539), who does not consider the confusion of the double dedication, says Romans would laugh at the suggestion of aristocracy that Lucretius makes about Memmius.

18. So Lucretius assumes that because Caesar had been Pontifex Maximus since 63 B.C., he must be careful not to offend his religious scruples, a matter that troubled Caesar not at all. Memmius was equally indifferent.

19. Catullus 10 and 28 give him a bad character. Cicero's character sketch of him in *Brutus* 247 branded him as too intellectually lazy to make the most of his excellent abilities as an orator and man of letters. Modern scholars have concluded from history and the testimony of his contemporaries that he was a selfish, unprincipled man. D. W. Roller, *C.P.* 65 (1970) 246ff., judges that Memmius represents all the worst elements in Roman society and thinks Lucretius must have known what every one else knew about him, that he counts for so little in the poem that omission of his name would be negligible. Bignone, *Storia* II.454, gives bibliography of modern comments on Memmius.

20. Harpocrates, a form of the Egyptian god Horus, is often represented with finger on lips as a symbol of secrecy.

21. A coin of Memmius's son (Grueber, *Coins of the Roman Republic in the British Museum*, London 1970, III; pl. 49.7) gives him the title of "imperator," apparently legitimate, though probably based on some obscure battle in Bithynia. See T. Frank, *C.P.* 14 (1919) 286f.

22. See T. Frank, *C.P.* 14 (1919) 286f.

23. A tenth example (II.1080) often cited depends on an emendation and so is hardly worth quoting.

24. v.8: "dicendum est deus ille fuit, deus, inclute Memmi."
v.93: "quoniam naturam triplicem, tria corpore, Memmi."
v.164: "cetera de genere hoc adiungere et addere, Memmi."
v.1281f.: "nam tibi quo pacto ferri natura reperta
  sit facile est ipsi per te cognoscere, Memmi."

25. "Lucretius seems to have been strangely blind to his (Memmius's) defects of character" (Leonard and Smith 201). For Memmius as a writer, see Pliny, *Ep.* v.1.5 and Cicero, *Brutus* 247.

26. For discussion of Lucretius I.49 in addition to Bailey's notes.

see Elder, *T.A.P.A.* 85 (1954) 88, on the Proem and the
"unfinished state of the poem."

27. Places where the attitude of Lucretius seems careful in this
regard are 1.50-53, 80-83, 102-109.

28. Sandbach, *C.R.* 54 (1940) 77.

29. Sinker, *Introduction to Lucretius*, Cambridge 1937, xviiif.

30. Cicero, at least, neglected to mention it to him. See above,
Chapter V, p. 99.

Bibliography

Alfonsi, L., *Poetae novi*, Como [1945].

Allen, W., Jr., "On the Friendship of Lucretius with Memmius," *C.P.* 33 (1938) 167-81.

Allen, W. S., *Vox Latina*, Cambridge 1965.

Amory, A., "Obscura de re lucida carmina: Science and Poetry in *De Rerum Natura*," *Yale Cl. St.* 21 (1969) 143-68.

Aulus Gellius, *Attic Nights*, J. C. Rolfe, trans., London and New York 1927-28.

Baehrens. See Catullus, C. Valerius.

Bailey. See Lucretius Carus.

Bieber, M., *The Greek and Roman Theatre*, 2nd ed., Princeton 1961.

Bignone, E., *Storia della litteratura latina*, Florence [1945-51].

Boyancé, P., *Lucrèce et l'epicurisme*, Paris 1963.

Butler. See Quintilian.

Catullus, C. Valerius, *Carmina*, R.A.B. Mynors, ed., Oxford 1958.

Catulli Veronensis, *Liber*, E. Baehrens, ed., Leipzig 1893.

———, G. Friedrich, ed., Leipzig and Berlin 1908.

———, L. Schwabe, ed., Berlin 1886.

Chevallier, R., "La celtique du Pô," *Latomus* 21 (1962) 356-70.

———, "La romanisation de l'Italie du Nord," *Rev. Belge* 43 (1965) 62-71.

Chilver, G.E.F., *Cisalpine Gaul*, Oxford 1941.

Ciceronis, M. Tullius, *Ad Q. Fratrem Epistolarum Libri tres*, H. Sjögren, ed., Göteborg and Leipzig 1911.

———, *Brutus*, G. L. Hendrickson, trans., Cambridge, Mass. and London 1952.

———, *De Oratore*, H. Rackham, ed. and trans., Cambridge, Mass. and London 1959.

———, *Letters*, R. Y. Tyrrell and L. C. Purser, eds., Hildesheim 1969.

Ciceronis, M. Tullius, *Orator*, H. M. Hubbell, ed., Cambridge, Mass. and London 1939.

Commager, H. S., Jr., "Lucretius' Interpretation of the Plague," *H.S.C.P.* 62 (1957) 105-18.

————, *The Odes of Horace. A Critical Study*, New Haven 1962.

Conway, R. S., Whatmough, J. P., Johnson, S. E., *The Prae-Italic Dialects of Italy*, Cambridge, Mass. 1933.

Cooper, C. G., *An Introduction to the Latin Hexameter*, Melbourne [1958].

Craig, J. D., " 'Counterpoint' in English and Latin Verse," *C.R.* 60 (1946) 14-17.

Cutt, T., "Meter and Diction in Catullus' Hendecasyllabics," diss. University of Chicago 1936.

Dale, F. R., "Caesar and Lucretius," *Greece and Rome*, Ser. 2, 5 (1958) 181-82.

D'Alton, J. R., *Roman Literary Theory and Criticism*, New York 1962.

Deutsch, R. E., *The Pattern of Sound in Lucretius*, Bryn Mawr 1939.

De Witt, N. C., *Roman Epicureanism*, Royal Society of Canada Transactions 1941.

Diehl, E., "De '*m*' finali epigraphica," *Jahrbücher f. class. Phil.*, Suppl. xxv, Leipzig 1899, 1-327.

Dudley, D. R., ed., *Lucretius (Studies in Latin Literature and its Influence)*, London [1965].

Duff, J. W., *A Literary History of Rome from the Origins to the Close of the Golden Age*, New York 1960.

————, *A Literary History of Rome in the Silver Age*, New York 1960.

Elder, J. P., "Notes on Some Conscious and Subconscious Elements in Catullus' Poetry," *H.S.C.P.* 60 (1951) 101-36.

Ellis, R., *A Commentary on Catullus*, 2nd ed., Oxford 1889.

Ernout. See Lucretius Carus, T.

Ewbank, W. W., *The Poems of Cicero*, London 1933.

Ewins, U., "The Early Colonisation of Cisalpine Gaul," *P.B.SR.*, N.S. 7 (1952) 54-71.

Fairclough. See Vergilius Maro.

Farrington, B., *The Faith of Epicurus*, London [1967].

————, "Form and Purpose in the *De Rerum Natura*," in Dudley, *Lucretius*, 19-34.

Ferguson, J., "Catullus and Cicero," *Latomus* 25 (1966) 871-72.

————, "Catullus and Horace," *A.J.P.* 77 (1956) 1-18.

Ferrero, L., *Poetica nuova in Lucrezio*, Florence [1949].

Fordyce, C. J., *Catullus, a Commentary*, Oxford 1961.

Frank, T., *Catullus and Horace*, New York 1965 [1928].

————, "Cicero and the Poetae Novi," *A.J.P.* 40 (1919) 396-415.

————, ed., *An Economic Survey of Ancient Rome*, Baltimore 1933-40.

————, *Vergil*, Oxford 1922.

Friedländer, P., "Pattern of Sound and Atomistic Theory in Lucretius," *A.J.P.* 62 (1941) 16-34.

Garrod, H. W., "Elision in Hendecasyllables," *Journal of Philology* 30 (1907) 90-94.

Gelzer, M., *Caesar, der Politiker und Staatsman*, Wiesbaden 1960.

Giussani, C., *T. Lucreti Cari. De rerum natura libri sex* (*Studi Lucreziani*, Vol. 1), Turin 1896-98.

Goold, G. P., "A New Text of Catullus," *Phoenix* 12 (1958) 93-116.

Grenier, A., "La Gaule romaine," in Frank, *An Economic Survey of Ancient Rome*, III, 379-644.

Hardie, W. R., *Res Metrica: An Introduction to the Study of Greek & Roman Versification*, Oxford 1920.

Harrington, K. P., ed., *The Roman Elegiac Poets*, Norman, Oklahoma [1968].

Havelock, E. A., *The Lyric Genius of Catullus*, Oxford 1939.

Hendrickson. See Cicero, *Brutus*.

————, "Horace and Valerius Cato [I]," *C.P.* 11 (1916) 249-69; "II," *C.P.* 12 (1917) 77-92; "III," *C.P.* 12 (1917) 329-50.

Herescu, N. I., ed., *Ovidiana. Recherches sur Ovide*, Paris 1958.

Herrmann, L., "Catulle et Lucrèce," *Latomus* 15 (1956) 465-80.

Holmes, T.R.E., *Caesar's Conquest of Gaul*, Oxford 1911.

Hubbell. See Cicero, *Orator*.

Keil, H., *Grammatici Latini*, Leipzig 1857-80.

Kenney, E. J., "Nequitiae poeta," in Herescu, *Ovidiana*, 201-209.

Kent, R. G., *The Sounds of Latin, Language*, Suppl. XII, September 1932.

Kent, R. G., and Sturtevant, E. H., "Elision and Hiatus in Latin Prose and Verse," *T.A.P.A.* 46 (1915) 129-55.

Knight, W.F.J., *Poetic Inspiration—an Approach to Virgil*, London 1946.

———, "Ovid's Metre and Rhythm," in Herescu, *Ovidiana*, 106-20.

———, *Roman Virgil*, 2nd ed., London [1944].

Last, H., and Gardner, R., "The Enfranchisement of Italy," *Cambridge Ancient History* IX, chap. VII.

Lee, M. O., "Illustrative Elisions in Catullus," *T.A.P.A.* 93 (1962) 144-53.

Leonard and Smith. See Lucretius Carus, T.

Lindsay, W. M., *Early Latin Verse*, Oxford 1922.

———, *The Latin Language*, Oxford 1894.

Lord, F., *Roman Pronunciation of Latin*, Boston 1894.

Lucretius Carus, T. *De Rerum Natura*. Bailey, C., ed., Oxford 1947.

———, A. Ernout, ed., 9th ed., Paris 1955-56.

———, W. E. Leonard and S. B. Smith, eds., Madison, Wisconsin 1942.

———, W. A. Merrill, ed., New York 1907.

———, H.A.J. Munro, ed., 4th ed., Cambridge 1893.

———, E. Paratore and U. Pizzani, eds., Rome 1960.

Mackail, J. W., trans., *The Aeneid of Vergil*, Oxford 1930.

MacKay, L. A., "On 'Patavinity,' " *C.P.* 38 (1943) 44-45.

Maguiness, W. S., "The Language of Lucretius," in Dudley, *Lucretius*, 69-93.

Marouzeau, J., *La prononciation du latin*, Paris 1931.

Marx, F., "Der Dichter Lucretius," *Neue Jahrb. kl. A.* 8 (1899) 532-48.

Meadows, G. K., "Hiatus and Vocalic Quality in Classical and Vulgar Latin," *C.P.* 41 (1946) 226-29.

Merrill, W. A., "The Lucretian Hexameter," *Univ. Cal. Stud. Cl. Phil.* 5 (1922) 253-96.

———, "Lucretius and Cicero," *C.R.* 10 (1890) 19.

———, see also Lucretius Carus.

Mewaldt, J., "Lucretius Carus (17)," Pauly-Wissowa, *Realencyclopädie* XIII, 1927.

Michels, A. K., "Lucretius, Clodius and Magna Mater," in *Melanges d'archéologie, d'épigraphie, et d'histoire offerts à Jérôme Carcopino*, [Paris] 1966, 675-79.

————, "Lucretius and the 6th Book of the *Aeneid*," *A.J.P.* 65 (1944) 135-48.

Munro. See Lucretius Carus.

Naughtin, V. P., "Metrical Patterns in Lucretius' Hexameters," *C.Q.* N.S. 2 (1952) 152-67.

Needham, P., trans., *Caesar, Politician and Statesman* (M. Gelzer), Oxford 1968.

Niedermann, M., *Précis de phonétique historique du latin*, Paris 1931.

Norden, E., *P. Vergilius Maro, Aeneis Buch VI*, Stuttgart 1957.

Oldfather, W. A., "The Most Extreme Case of Elision in the Latin Language?" *C.J.* 38 (1942-43) 478-79.

Otis, B., *Ovid as an Epic Poet*, Cambridge 1966.

Paratore. See Lucretius Carus.

Pascal, C. B., "The Cults of Cisalpine Gaul," *Coll. Latomus* 75, Brussels 1964.

Platnauer, M., "Elision of *atque* in Roman Poetry," *C.Q.* 42 (1948) 91-93.

————, *Latin Elegiac Verse*, Cambridge 1951.

Quinn, K., *The Catullan Revolution*, Cambridge [1969].

Quintilian, *Institutio Oratoria*, Butler, H. E., trans., London and New York 1921-22 (Loeb edition).

Rackham. See Cicero, *De Oratore*.

Rand, E. K., "Catullus and the Augustans," *H.S.C.P.* 17 (1906) 15-30.

Regenbogen, O., *Lukrez; seine Gestalt in seinem Gedicht*, Leipzig and Berlin 1932.

Roberts, L., *A Concordance of Lucretius* (*Agon* Supplement 1968), [Berkeley 1968].

Roberts, W. R., ed. and trans., *Demetrius on Style*, Cambridge 1902.

————, ed. and trans., *Dionysius of Halicarnassus, On Literary Composition*, London 1910.

Robson, D. O., "The Samnites in the Po Valley," *C.J.* 29 (1933-34) 599-608.

Roller, D. W., "Gaius Memmius, Patron of Lucretius," *C.P.* 65 (1970) 246-48.

Ross, D. O., *Style and Tradition in Catullus*, Cambridge, Mass. 1969.

Bibliography

Salmon, E. T., "S.M.P.E.," in Herescu, *Ovidiana* 3-20.

——, *Samnium and the Samnites*, Cambridge 1967.

Sandbach, F. H., "*Lucreti poemata* and the Poet's Death," *C.R.* 54 (1940) 72-77.

Sedgwick, W. B., "Catullus' Elegiacs," *Mnemosyne* Ser. 4, 3 (1950) 64-69.

Sellar, W. Y., *The Roman Poets of the Republic*, Oxford 1881.

Shipley, F. W., "Hiatus, Elision, Caesura, in Virgil's Hexameter," *T.A.P.A.* 55 (1924) 137-58.

Siedow, A., "de elisionis aphaeresis hiatus usu in hexametris latinis," diss. Greifswald 1911.

Sihler, E. G., "Lucretius and Cicero," *T.A.P.A.* 28 (1897) 42-54.

Sikes, E. E., *Lucretius—Poet and Philosopher*, Cambridge 1936.

Smith, K. F., *The Elegies of Albius Tibullus*, New York [1913].

Soubiran, J., *L'élision dans la poésie latine*, Paris 1966.

Tait, J.I.M., "Philodemus' Influence on the Latin Poets," diss. Bryn Mawr 1941.

Taylor, L. R., "Caesar's Early Career," *C.P.* 36 (1941) 113-32.

——, "Lucretius on the Theatre," *Phoenix*, Suppl. 1, Toronto 1952, 147-51.

——, *Party Politics in the Age of Caesar*, Berkeley 1949.

——, *The Voting Districts of the Roman Republic*, Rome 1960.

Todd, O. J., "Sense and Sound in Classical Poetry," *C.Q.* 36 (1942) 29-39.

Toynbee, A. J., *Hannibal's Legacy*, Oxford 1965.

Traglia, A., *Note su Cicerone critico e traduttore*, Rome 1947.

——, *Sulla formazione spirituale di lucrezio*, Rome 1948.

Trencsényi-Waldapfel, I., "Cicéron et Lucrèce," *Acta antiqua academiae scientiarum Hungaricae*, 1958, 321-83.

Tyrrell and Purser. See Cicero, *Letters*.

Valle, G. della, *Tito Lucrezi Caro e l'epicureismo campano*, Naples 1933.

Vergilius Maro, Publius, *Aeneid*, ed., H. R. Fairclough, Cambridge, Mass. and London 1950.

Waszink, J. H., "Lucretius and Poetry," *Mededel. Nederl. Akad. van Wetensch.* 17, 1954, no. 8.

West, D. A., *The Imagery and Poetry of Lucretius*, Edinburgh 1969.

Whatmough, J., *The Foundations of Roman Italy*, London 1937.

Williams, G., *Tradition and Originality in Roman Poetry*, Oxford 1968.

Wiseman, T. P., *Cinna the Poet and other Roman Essays*, Leicester 1974.

Wilkinson, L. P., *The Georgics of Vergil. A Critical Survey*, Cambridge 1969.

———, *Golden Latin Artistry*, Cambridge 1963.

———, *Ovid Recalled*, Cambridge 1955.

Index

Aeneadae, 106, 108

Aeneadum, 103, 108; first used by Lucretius, 103; *Aeneadum genetrix*, 52, 102, 106

Aeneas, 17, 38, 86, 103, 107

Aeneid, 15, 19, 20, 36, 65, 69, 79, 86, 108, 118 n. 16, 120 n. 39, 122 n. 50, 129 n. 8, 131 n. 33, 133 n. 19

Aetna, Mt., 35-36, 49

Alfenus Varus, 11, 28

Allen, W. S., 123 n. 54

Amafinius, Gaius, 99-100

Amaror, borrowed by Virgil, 70; invented by Lucretius, 70

Anchises, 38, 103

Ancus Marcius, 102

Angat, used by Lucretius and Virgil, 69

Antenor, 36

Aquileia, 104, 137 n. 3

Aratus, 16

Archias, Aulus Licinius, 6. *See also Pro Archias*

Arpinum, 5-6, 125 n. 18

Arrius, Quintus, 25, 28-29, 30

aspirate, 25, 30

Athens, 114; Greek of, as standard, 6, 9, 26; Epicurus's house, 99, 114

Atticus, Titus Pomponius, 47, 88, 90, 92, 93, 97, 99, 125 n. 14, 136 n. 16

Augustans, 3, 14, 71, 100, 126 n. 28, 127 n. 38, 129 n. 8

Augustus, Gaius Octavius, 103; age of, 20, 115

Bacchus, 45, 133 n. 17

Bailey, C., 49, 54, 67, 130 n. 28, 132 ns. 1, 12, 134 n. 30

Beneventum, 6

Bibaculus, Marcus Furius, 11

Bignone, E., 90

Bithynia, 23, 107

Boii, 11

borrowing: Catullus from Lucretius, 47, 65; Cicero from Lucretius, 134 n. 27; Horace from Lucretius, 119-20 n. 30; Latin speakers from Gauls, 11; Lucretius from Catullus, 47, 65; Ovid from Catullus, 121-22 n. 50; Ovid from northerners, 17; Quintilian from Lucretius, 9; Virgil from Lucretius, 70. *See also* echoing

Britain, 105

Brutus, 5, 8-9, 12, 13, 16, 28, 29, 117 ns. 1, 8, 10, 120 ns. 32, 34, 38, 42, 124-25 n. 9

149

Library of Congress Cataloging in Publication Data

Holland, Louise Adams.
  Lucretius and the Transpadanes.
  Bibliography: p.
  Includes index.
    1. Latin language—Provincialisms—Italy, Northern.
  2. Latin language—Pronunciation.   3. Lucretius
Carus, Titus—Criticism and interpretation.
  I. Title.
PR2698.I8H6   471   79-1415
ISBN 0-691-06401-6